Another Kind of Witness

Flowers placed by survivors at base of Liberty Bell, Sunday afternoon, April 21

Another Kind of Witness

Bernard F. Stehle

Foreword by Geoffrey Hartman

Afterword by Sister Gloria Coleman

The Jewish Publication Society

Philadelphia / New York / Jerusalem   5748 / 1988

"In the world of the Holocaust, the ordinary was extraordinary, and that is why we are here to honor the Danish people."

Roman Kent, Survivor, Chairman of the Board of the American Gathering
of Jewish Holocaust Survivors, on presenting the "Shofar of Freedom"
Award to the Government and People of Denmark

"We were grateful to be able to do our simple human duty."

His Excellency Eigil Jørgensen, Ambassador of Denmark
to the United States, on accepting the "Shofar of Freedom" Award on behalf
of the Government and People of Denmark

Philadelphia, April 22, 1985

Designed by ADRIANNE ONDERDONK DUDDEN

To my lifelong friend and inspiration

Nora Levin

student and historian of the Holocaust
devoted teacher and educator
friend to all survivors
and to the

**Association of Jewish Holocaust Survivors
in Philadelphia**

and

The American Gathering of Jewish Holocaust Survivors

I dedicate this book

"Monument to the Six Million Jewish Martyrs" by Nathan Rapaport, photographed at dusk on the day of the memorial service

Foreword

Photographs are minimal icons, especially important for a people who have no icons, a people whose art is concentrated on biblical interpretation, literature, and the crafting of ceremonial objects. Yet, by a bad break of history (mother of bad breaks), the photographs that have imprinted themselves most vividly on our imagination are those that tell of a destruction so intense and catastrophic that we single it out by the special word *Holocaust*. If the prohibition against graven images is linked to a fear of desecrating the divine image, and if humankind is made in the image of God, then what is recorded by photographs of the Holocaust, and seems to contaminate the camera itself, could not be more terrible.

But the photographs we usually live with, and which help us to remember, are the ones first mentioned by the author of this moving book, a Christian of German descent. He casts his project of documenting the Inaugural Gathering of American Jewish Holocaust Survivors (in Philadelphia, April 20–23, 1985) as a letter to his young children. "Dear Justine and Mark, You know how we love looking at old family photographs together? Well, here's one of me taken in 1946 when we lived on Anchor Street . . . I was born during that war and was just three years old in April 1945, when the Nazi concentration camps were liberated. An estimated total of eleven to twelve million people perished in the camps, and in the many other murderous actions taken by the Nazis against specially targeted groups. . . . Nearly six million of those murdered were Jews, and of those over a million were children as Uncle Ed, Aunt Judy, and I were at the time. And as you are now. It is the death of those children that especially haunts me."

The impulse that motivated Bernard Stehle is also the one that led the survivors to organize and meet together, forty years after Liberation. Could they find a way of telling the world, but also—above all—their own children, what happened? Is there a legacy, other than sheer terror, pain, and disability, that can be passed on to the second and already to the third generation? Can they be witnesses in the years still left, now that most who survived are approaching the full term of human life?

Alas, too many photographs in the family album of survivors are missing. We can imagine those domestic scenes, perhaps awkwardly posed: the mother (pregnant) holding another child; the father in formal regalia; the *Firma* or business; the absurdly clad bathing beauties; a meeting of the Bund or the Bar Kochba sports club; a family picnic in the countryside; the child with a *Tüte* (a cornucopia of sweets) on his first day in school. They are missing, or few in number; or they evoke, because of those who did not survive, an overwhelming sadness. For the families who came to Philadelphia there is only a precarious continuity with the past: The continuity is all in the future, for the sake of which they gathered as an Assembly. Bernard Stehle's album is therefore a kind of restitution. It shows the restored and larger family, the thousands of survivors and friends who created these icons as part of a necessary ritual of commemoration. It bears witness not only to a destruction they have vowed not to forget but to their rebirth in this generous country and in a city where, two years later, the Bicentennial of the Constitution would be celebrated.

Nothing, you will say, can make up for the lost album. That is true, of course. How often witnesses who tell their stories for video taping hold up a faded or torn snapshot! Nothing can bring back the family world that was destroyed. There are, in Stehle's album, impressive pictures of Processions, Ceremonies, Exhibits, Monuments, Dignitaries. But I do not think we seek this new, heroic mode. We barely tolerate, in fact, what moves us more deeply—because it moves us so deeply: that simple photograph of Sam Rusinik, survivor of Bedzia, waiting expectantly with a camera around his neck, or of a fragile Jan Karski (the Polish courier who tried to persuade the Allies to intervene against the massacre of the Jews) being helped from the podium. We don't seek such images, heroic or natural, yet we must have them: every face, every story to go with it, every sign of continuity, new life, and an active American community. Perhaps we need them too much, as if to convince ourselves that what happened will not, cannot, happen again.

These are not beautiful photographs in the conventional sense. They are documents, as the author says; yet they are suffused by his own intense quest for identity, which somehow parallels the quest of the survivors. Each face is, or seems, familiar, and all who appear are conscious not only of testifying but also of looking for a link to the past. Their portraits are statements of identity. Thus the many names, badges, banners: Etta Hecht (Levin), wearing, in addition to her lovely smile, the badges "Never Again," "Free Wallenberg," and a namecard with her double provenance: Pottstown, Pa., and Kovno, Lithuania; or Isaac Shneyderman, suppressing tears, holding up a picture of three family members, two of them children, Russian Jews from Kiev killed at Babi Yar—their picture, held this way, resembling a religious icon. It is all in the open. The images say: We are free, we have come out of bondage; we are among brothers and sisters in a country we trust; we are no longer afraid to show ourselves and be counted.

It is all in the open. And yet, necessarily, much remains hidden. Through the narratives that accompany the photographs—small oral histories epitomizing the author's conversations with the survivors—we learn of a wealth of experience and fated personal history that these images, strong as they are, cannot encompass. We also learn about the emotion of the children of survivors, for whom this meeting seems to have been as crucial as for the survivors themselves: Many have no extended families; many are working through difficult feelings ("guilt, anger, sense of responsibility . . ."). For some, however, the Gathering was a kind of breakthrough, the solidarity of it encouraging fuller and more intimate conversation in the family.

What is most affecting here? A certain blend of loneliness and determination. I am not sure the photographer-author's aim could ever be accomplished: He wanted to reach out, through this book, and create a healing dialogue that would also embrace non-Jews like himself and children like his own. One honors that aim and his clear sense that "the Holocaust touches all humankind." The photographs, however, perhaps because of something in the nature of photography itself, rarely convey a sense of togetherness. A picture of survivors singing Yiddish folksongs catches it in the form of spirited nostalgia. Mostly, however, the sad solemnity of recovered memories isolates each person, turns them inward, and invests their images with a pensive, almost monumental aura. A tension between the collective setting of high ritual and the distinctive bearing of each individual in this setting, points up rather than subdues what cannot be healed: a deep loss, like that of a child or parent or dearest friend. Three from Auschwitz attend the Assembly and someone happens to notice how close their camp numbers are: 174247, 174248, 174250. The joy of mutual recognition is great but that missing number symbolizes what is always subliminally there: the absence of a close friend, shot while attempting to escape from the Auschwitz death march early in 1945. Though we have need of this book, we continue to evoke the missing photographs, real or imaginary, taken before the destruction. Is the loneliness I sense in these icons like that absence: an invisible tear or crease, recorded by the sensitive photographer?

Yet images like these do have a healing effect—in a somewhat unexpected sense. The persecutors took photographs shamelessly: Indeed, the archives and halls of our memorial museums display *their* pictures of Jewish captivity, destitution, degradation. How ironic that the victimizers provide the best evidence against themselves, in their arrogant certainty of documenting the doom of the Jews. How sad that such images come, almost all of them, from the murderous source. *Another Kind of Witness* directs itself against such picturebooks of the murderers. Most of us have seen those sad, anonymous faces looking fleetingly at us from Nazi archival footage: a young boy, his arms raised in an adult gesture of surrender; a girl framed by the closing door of a boxcar; bearded elders rounded up, paraded, humiliated; men and women, naked, taking their last steps; "Eternal Jew" mugshots of supposed racial and criminal features. It is against these images of inhumanity, and for the victims they degrade, that the present album testifies, replacing anonymity with name upon name, looking tenderly at each person or group, and, yes, not afraid to be proud and to proclaim how far they have come: "From Holocaust . . . To New Life." These are not triumphant pictures; they contain too much fragility amid the signs of celebration. But one is grateful to Bernard Stehle and the survivors for glimpses that affirm rather than deny the past and that suggest how everyone is "a child of the Holocaust period."

Geoffrey Hartman

Geoffrey Hartman, Revson Project Director of Yale's Video Archive for Holocaust Testimonies, has recently edited *Bitburg in Moral and Political Perspective* (Indiana) and *Midrash and Literature* (Yale).

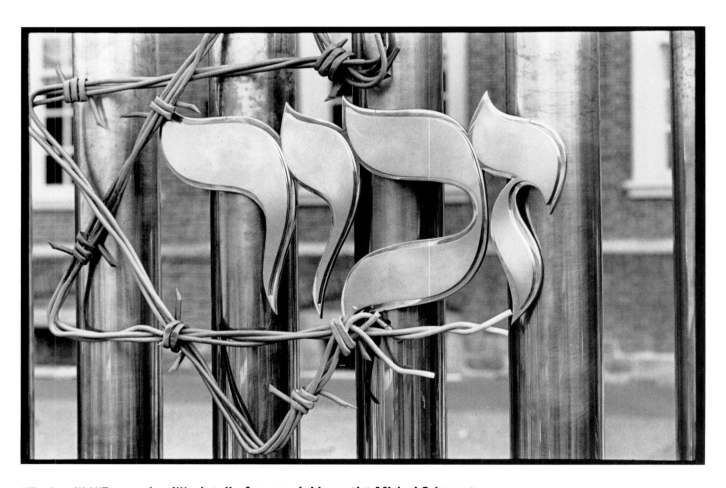

"Zachor!" ("Remember!"), detail of memorial by artist Michel Schwartz

Author's Preface

"As long as there is denial, there can be no healing."

Itka Zygmuntowicz
Survivor of Auschwitz

All but a few of the photographs in this book were made during the four days of the American Gathering of Jewish Holocaust Survivors, which met in Philadelphia in April 1985, the fortieth anniversary of the liberation of the Nazi concentration camps. The text is a letter to my children that was inspired by a question put to me by my eleven-year-old son one night a year after the Gathering.

It was a Sunday in May, and Mark and I were sitting in one of our favorite restaurants at the conclusion of a weekend together, two weeks before the opening of the first exhibition of "Another Kind of Witness." The last of the photographs had been mounted and framed, but I still had not settled on a text to accompany them when Mark slid his marble copybook across the table and asked me to test him on his social studies. As I picked up the open notebook, my attention was drawn immediately to the heading: "Another War"—Mark's notation for World War II. I framed my questions to accord with two of the notes.

"Who was Adolf Hitler?"

"Leader of the Germans," Mark answered.

"What did he do?"

"He killed a lot of Jews."

That was the extent of his notes on Hitler and the Jews. It was already more than I had been taught in all my years of elementary and high school education back in the fifties. "Do you know how many Jews were killed?" I ventured carefully.

Mark looked blank.

"Almost six million," I said.

I could feel him thinking during the long pause that followed. "When?"

"*When?*" I echoed, uncertain what information he wanted. "About seven years," I continued, "mostly between 1941 and—"

"But if it was going on for that long," Mark interrupted, "why didn't anybody do something about it?"

I looked at him without a word for several seconds, then looked away as I began struggling with the explanations I had learned long since leaving school. But they wouldn't do, and the excuses, qualifications, exceptions trailed off finally as I faced my son again, speechless.

The very next morning I was trying to figure out a way to contact survivors for the kind of text I now knew I wanted to write. I had never before spoken to either of my children about the Holocaust. And neither Mark nor his older sister, Justine, were among the many students from area schools who had gone to the Gathering a year before and learned about the Holocaust directly from survivors. The letter that I decided to write to my children would tell them about the Holocaust in the voices and stories of the survivors themselves, complementing the photographs I had taken of them at the Gathering. By bringing the Gathering to Mark and Justine in this way, I hoped to make the terrible statistics of the Holocaust seem less "unreal" to them and to develop a human context in which to respond to my son's question of the night before.

Contacting the survivors loomed as a problem, because I had so few of their addresses and telephone numbers. So many had attended the Gathering that I spoke at length with fewer than ten people over the entire four days—though I had met hundreds, eighty of whom were featured in the photographs about to go on display. I was wondering how survivors would react to my pursuing the abbreviated exchanges of a year earlier, when the seemingly obvious solution as to how to get in touch with them finally presented itself—the nametags! I began to look quickly through the photographs. Only the home city and state appeared on the tags in addition to each registrant's name, but that could be a start. I kept looking. Although some names were out of focus or covered in part by a lapel or other fold of clothing, most of the survivors were wearing their nametags—and the names were readable.

For the next ten days I telephoned survivors in cities all over the United States and abroad. Information operators were able to provide almost all of the numbers I needed. I now was able to speak at length with the survivors whom a year before I had engaged only briefly in the course of taking more than two thousand photographs. I made notes as they unfolded their stories, often tearfully and with long pauses as they reached back for a detail or felt again how little the pain had subsided, even after so many years.

The exhibition opened on schedule. The open letter to my children that accompanied the photographs related some of the stories and feelings of the survivors, their children, and their friends who attended that weekend. I tried also to describe the events and historical significance of the Gathering and to explore my own motivations for having participated. Another show followed six months later, with additional stories. This book version of "Another Kind of Witness" includes a selection of these and further accounts garnered during the past two years— through phone calls and visits with survivors and their children, letters, tape-recorded interviews, and, especially, meetings with my Philadelphia friends in the Association of Jewish Holocaust Survivors. The accounts of volunteers at the Gathering, program participants, and liberators are also included. And the conversations continue.

"Was it really me?" Joseph Fishman, a survivor of Auschwitz, said recently, recalling the skeleton he had become by the time of his liberation from Bergen-Belsen in May 1945. "It was so out of this world, so out of the natural order of things: How could it have happened?"

It is the question that we all ask ourselves when the Holocaust first confronts us with its unparalleled evil—and we continue to struggle with it in our roles as citizens, educators, parents. And, just as children of survivors have needed their parents to share their pain—despite the difficulty, despite their long silence—so too the photographs and letter that follow are my attempt at beginning with my children the kind of dialogue about the Holocaust that we non-Jews also need to have. The very reasons this is hard to do—the disturbing contemporary implications, the appalling historical record, and the personal vulnerability each of us brings to such an effort—are the very reasons it is necessary. Fortunately, survivors themselves show us the way, as do our children.

"Why didn't anybody do something about it?" I had felt challenged to the core of my being that night by my son, his compassion unencumbered by ideology and the host of other defenses and projections we acquire. "What would *you* have done, Dad?"—I had felt him asking—"What are you doing *now*?"

Philadelphia, September 1987
In the 200th anniversary month of the
signing of the Constitution of the United States

Another Kind of Witness

Self, 1946

Dear Mark and Justine,

You know how we love looking at old family photographs together? Well, here's one of me taken in 1946 when we lived on Anchor Street. I was four years old at the time, less than a year after the end of World War II—the war that you learned something about last year in fifth grade, Mark, and that you are studying now, Justine. I was just three years old in April 1945, when the inmates of the Nazi concentration camps were being liberated in Europe. An estimated total of eleven to twelve million people perished in those camps and in the many other murderous actions taken by the Nazis against specially targeted groups, certain civilian populations, and prisoners of war. Nearly six million of those who perished were Jews, and of these over a million were children as Uncle Ed, Aunt Judy, and I were at the time. And as you are now.

It is the death of those children that especially haunts me. I have found it very hard to deal with the irony of fate that had me, a Catholic child of German descent, happily riding my tricycle in Philadelphia—carefree as the summer breeze!—while hundreds of thousands of my childhood peers across the ocean were being thrown into fire pits, gassed, or murdered in other unthinkable ways simply because, unlike myself, they were Jewish.

Although I am not Jewish, I consider myself a child of the Holocaust period, and so I try to provide another kind of witness, along with those who actually suffered through and survived the Holocaust. That book I gave you, Justine—*Night*, by Elie Wiesel—is one I use in the college writing courses I teach. I try to help students connect their lives to the deepest issues of our times, of which the Holocaust is surely one. Elie Wiesel was fifteen—just your age, Justine—when he was deported by cattle car to Auschwitz with his mother, father, and three sisters. You are ready for his story now, though in a sense one can never be ready for it. We need to discuss these hard things together, and to attend to what is going on even now in the world, for genocide and mass killings are not only of the past and not only of the Jews. The Holocaust touches all humankind. Acknowledging that fact—raising our own individual consciousness—is the first action any of us can take to begin making the world a better place for all. Thus we keep solidarity with the dead as well as with those who bear living witness to the inhumanity they have suffered and dare not forget. This was the mission of the several thousand who attended the American Gathering of Jewish Holocaust Survivors in April 1985, the fortieth anniversary of their liberation from the concentration camps.

I went to the Gathering to document that historic weekend, but even more, I realized later, to confront my own personal history. For as a child I had lost over a million brothers and sisters in a Slaughter of the Innocents of which I had no awareness. As an adult, however, I had come to understand my roots as an American, a Christian, and a fourth-generation German, and thus the burden of my own historical responsibility for what had been done—and what had not been done.

This was the pain that I took with me to the Gathering along with all my cameras and film. As the weekend unfolded, and I met more and more survivors, I became aware that some part of me hoped to meet a child survivor—one who had been three years old in April 1945, someone whose pain I might now be able to touch, someone to whom I might be able to say, across the years from our separate childhoods: Your life helps heal mine.

Here are some of the photographs and stories of the people I met during that extraordinary weekend, a kind of family album for us to return to again and again as we seek together to understand the Holocaust and its lessons for all humankind. . . .

Beth El Choir of Cherry Hill, New Jersey . . .

. . . at welcoming reception, Saturday evening

Havdalah, evening of the welcoming reception

"We do not want to live in the past, but to keep the past living," said Abram Shnaper in his welcoming address at the Civic Center on April 20, following the chanting of *Havdalah* ("Separation"), the traditional Jewish ceremony that marks the conclusion of the Sabbath and the beginning of a new week. The ceremony that evening marked the beginning of four memorable days for the Jewish Holocaust survivors and their children who came to Philadelphia from all parts of the United States, and abroad, to participate in public acts of remembrance, commemoration, and appreciation.

Abram Shnaper's words held special meaning for him and his fellow survivors, evident that night in the faces of the children singing in the choir and in the sweetness of their voices raised in Hebrew song, for it is they who embodied the

Abram Shnaper delivering the welcoming address

very theme of the Gathering and the hope of all survivors: that the past will be kept alive—that the lessons of the Holocaust will be handed down from generation to generation, never to be forgotten. Abram, born in Vilna, the "Jerusalem of Lithuania," is one of the living witnesses whose involvement throughout the weekend demonstrated a special devotion to the task.

Abram and Luba Shnaper were married in Warsaw in 1947, two years after their liberation—Abram from a labor camp in Estonia, Luba from one in Germany. Both had survived the Vilna Ghetto while almost two thirds of the Jewish population of the city and its surrounding settlements had been slaughtered by the Nazis and their collaborators at Ponary, just outside the city. Between July and December of 1941 alone, over 48,000 were murdered there.

Abram had been jailed in one of the many round-ups of Jews and was about to be sent to Ponary when his mother, in desperation, appealed to a German soldier on the street to rescue her son. Luckily, she picked out a compassionate man who apparently was neither a Nazi nor a Nazi sympathizer. Spontaneously agreeing to help, he went directly to the prison and used the one strategy likely to have some effect on the SS authorities. (At first Hitler's personal security squad, the SS—*Schutzstaffeln*, or "Elite Guard"—had become a vast empire, comprising twelve departments, parts of which supervised and carried out the mass murder of the Jews, as at Ponary.) In a peremptory tone of voice to the SS officers in charge at the prison, the soldier declared that Abram was working for him: "This Jew is mine!

I need him!" It worked. Abram was released unharmed into the German's "custody." Once out of view of the authorities, the soldier would accept nothing for his help and was gone. While intervention of any kind was all too tragically the exception during the Holocaust, it was rarer still within the military. Even today Abram, president of the Association of Jewish Holocaust Survivors in Philadelphia, cannot recount this extraordinary incident without acknowledging a quiet astonishment, along with his indebtedness to a soldier of the regular German Army who risked his life to save a Jewish mother from her grief. Ironically, Abram, who nearly had been the first member of his family to fall victim to the Nazis, ultimately was the only one to survive the Holocaust.

At the welcoming reception I also met Chaya Ash-Fuhrman. She was a twenty-year-old actress living in Kishinev, Rumania, when the Russians occupied that country in 1940. In June 1941, when Germany attacked the Soviet Union, she and her parents were sent with other "untrusted citizens" (in Chaya's words) to labor camps deep inside Russia. Several weeks later, the Germans entered Kishinev, followed quickly by *Einsatzgruppen,* special killing squads of SS and their recruits, who began murdering the Jews. In just one ten-day stretch of continuous slaughter in July alone, they claimed over 14,000 victims. Although Chaya escaped that fate, she suffered terrible conditions during the five years she spent in a labor camp on the border of Afghanistan and Russia. "They dug big holes in the ground and put a roof on top—that's where we lived." Her father died from starvation, but Chaya and her mother survived severe malnutrition, boils, and malaria. Her only sibling, a brother, was sent to a different labor camp where his artistic talents were used to produce anti-fascist posters for Soviet propaganda against Germany. He also survived. In 1946 Chaya married a Polish Jew whom she had met in the labor camp. She thus was able to leave Russia that year and return to Poland in a postwar repatriation of citizens. In 1962 she came to the United States, where she resumed her acting career on the Yiddish stage.

Although Rabbi Irving Block of the New York Board of Rabbis is not himself a survivor, his life has been changed by close friendships with people who are, such as Joseph Tekulsky. "You can't really love another person until you understand something of their pain," Rabbi Block said. "I want to see their faces and to be confronted, to feel their pain in order to more fully participate in their joy—that's why I go to these meetings [of survivors]." Irving and Joseph have known each other since 1948, when they shared a bachelor's apartment in New York City with two of Joseph's other friends, also survivors.

Joseph had survived one of the most heroic acts of resistance during the war—the Warsaw Ghetto Uprising of April 1943. Determined not to enter the deportation columns—which, they had come to realize, led ultimately to the Treblinka death camp—about 1,200 Jewish fighters, mostly youths in their teens and early twenties, revolted. Using whatever arms they managed to smuggle into the ghetto or concoct themselves—pistols, hand grenades, homemade pipe bombs, Molotov cocktails, and a few rifles—they proceeded to astonish the Germans, indeed the world, by holding off some 2,500 German troops—armed with flame throwers, machine guns, and howitzers—for more than three weeks. Some resistance flickered on even after the ghetto had been essentially destroyed by the middle of May.

Although it was not the first Jewish armed resistance, the Warsaw Ghetto Uprising was the largest and most protracted, inspiring several uprisings elsewhere within the next year. Yet it failed to inspire any action in the world outside the ghettos and death camps: The murder of Jews continued unabated. Despite this, it was—and remains—a matter of pride for Jews that a single section of the Warsaw Ghetto, a fraction of a square mile in size, held out longer against the Nazis in the spring of 1943 than did all of Poland in the fall of 1939.

"L'Chaim!" Chaya Ash-Fuhrman at the reception

Joseph Tekulsky (l.) and Rabbi Block at the reception

Weeks later, in the final days of the burning ghetto, Joseph and his family were among the very last resisters flushed out by gas from their underground bunker. Deported to Treblinka, he was the only one of them who did not end up among the estimated 850,000 Jews murdered there. In a rare transport out of Treblinka, Joseph was one of 300 men sent to the Majdanek death camp; from there he was transferred from one labor camp to another before being liberated by American troops at Mauthausen, the extermination camp in Austria, in May 1945.

Selma and Peter Brothman with Joseph Fishman, survivor

One of the founders of the Warsaw Ghetto Resisters Organization, Joseph lives with his wife in Fort Lee, New Jersey. They have two children, both married, and two grandchildren. "We survivors can never forget, even if we wanted to," Joseph said to me. "But we must also not forget to enjoy life, too. There is a time to remember, and a time to rejoice in what we have accomplished since: in spite of Hitler, in spite of the Nazis, in spite of the Holocaust."

What they might learn from survivors led many Philadelphians to open their homes to those who otherwise might not have been able to come to the Gathering. "I wanted our children to meet someone who had gone through the Holocaust," Selma Brothman explained. Joseph Fishman's visit with the Brothmans has had a continuing effect on their lives. Natalie, age 9, has exchanged letters with him, and Selma now volunteers her time to interview survivors for the Holocaust Oral History Archive at Gratz College in Philadelphia. "I feel a link with my history," she says. "It's just luck that I was here, not there. It helps me not take things for granted."

Out of seven brothers and sisters and both parents deported from Sighet, Hungary (now Rumania) to Auschwitz in May 1944, only Joseph Fishman and his youngest sister survived. Teenagers at the time, they were liberated in April 1945 when British troops entered the Bergen-Belsen concentration camp, near Hanover in north-central Germany. The liberators were shocked and sickened by what they

Detail, "Monument to the Six Million Jewish Martyrs"

saw: over 12,000 unburied dead, and thousands of living skeletons among the 40,000 survivors, dozens dying every hour from disease and starvation. "When I got liberated, I couldn't even move," Joseph remembers. "I weighed only sixty pounds. We were just lying there on wooden bunks, waiting to die."

Today, Joseph Fishman, who wore a striped suit and hat to the Gathering as a reminder of his prison garb in the camps, is a retired tailor living in Montreal. Although a member of Canada's Association of Survivors of Nazi Oppression, he

Joel (l.), Meredith and David, grandchildren of survivors, at the monument

also understands those survivors who choose not to join associations nor to attend Gatherings. "The main reason people stay away is the pain and loss. It is too much. At first it was too painful for me as well, but now I *want* to come. I come to meet my fellow survivors, to share stories. We have to keep it alive." And not all the memories are painful, he adds, recalling the joys of his boyhood days with Elie Wiesel. "In those days," he says with laughter, "we had to make footballs from stuffed stockings! And we kicked the ball around in the street. We were happy."

On Sunday afternoon, the day after the welcoming reception, members of the general public joined several thousand survivors and their families and friends in a solemn *Yom Ha-Shoah* (Holocaust Remembrance Day) ceremony at the "Monument to the Six Million Jewish Martyrs," sculpted by Nathan Rapaport. Presented to the city in 1964 by the Federation of Jewish Agencies (FJA) and the Association of

Vladka and Benjamin Meed at the memorial service, Sunday

Jewish Holocaust Survivors in Philadelphia, it was the first public monument of its kind ever erected in North America. Standing below the towering bronze figures, three grandchildren of survivors presented a tableau of hope and deliverance as they quietly flanked a wreath that symbolized their own connection to those memorialized dead. "It wasn't fair that Hitler could be so mean just because they were Jews," said Joel Schoenbach, age 9, grandson of Abram and Luba Shnaper. "It makes me feel kind of angry at Hitler, and proud to represent all the children who died."

Meredith Okon, age 8, told me of her feelings that afternoon. "I felt good," she recalled, "and sad, because a lot of them were my family." At home she hears many stories about the ghettos and concentration camps. "My grandparents tell me a lot about it ... but I don't understand why they did it to us." And David Goldman, age 11, said recently, "It's really important that we remember. I'd feel the same way even if it happened to *any*body. We should all remember, and stick together as humans."

"Forty years ago we were abandoned," said Vladka Meed, survivor of the Warsaw Ghetto, in her keynote address to survivors and many others assembled at the *Yom Ha-Shoah* ceremony. Two years after Hitler came to power in Germany,

Survivors and their families at the memorial service

all German Jews were stripped of their citizenship and other legal and human rights by the infamous Nuremberg Laws of 1935. Like most non-Jewish Germans, many other European peoples allowed their deeply ingrained religious prejudices and cultural stereotypes to be exploited by the Nazis as their towns came under German occupation. It was because Hitler found willing audiences for his vicious racial accusations that he was able to orchestrate a campaign of propaganda and terror against the Jews, whom he blamed for all of Germany's—and by extension the world's—political and economic woes. Verbal dehumanization was followed by countless varieties of public ridicule, physical intimidation, and violence in broad daylight. Anti-Jewish measures included the exclusion of Jews from normal social

Photos of Abram Rubinowicz family, Lodz Ghetto, 1940

and political life, the burning of books and synagogues, and finally ghettos, mobile killing squads, and deportations to concentration (slave labor and extermination) camps. Most citizens of Germany and of the countries conquered by Germany responded to the persecution of the Jews with indifference, passive cooperation, or, in many cases, enthusiastic participation. The educated as well as the uneducated were taken in. Comparatively few voices were raised, individually or collectively, against this creeping, then galloping, process of genocide.

"Yes, we will remember with gratitude and respect the deceny of the few, of

Listening to Vladka Meed's keynote address

Television crew at the memorial service, filming Isaac Shneyderman . . .

some righteous people and nations," said Vladka Meed. She had joined the Jewish underground resistance during the first days of Hitler's invasion of Poland in 1939, when she was seventeen years old. Able to pass as an "Aryan" (non-Jew) because of her light hair and blue eyes, she became one of the main couriers from the Warsaw Ghetto, smuggling in weapons to the Jewish Fighting Organization (JFO), aiding partisans in the forests and woods, identifying Christians who were willing to risk hiding Jewish women and children, and carrying forged identification papers and money to Jews already in hiding. She tells her story in a book, *On Both Sides of the Wall,* first published in 1948, in which she describes the idealism and extraordinary resourcefulness of such heroes as Mordecai Anielewicz and Yitzhak Zuckerman, leaders of the JFO during the darkest days of the ghetto.

"Forty years ago we were abandoned." Even in the United States, members of the State Department and others in positions of highest authority knew full well by the fall of 1942 that the Jews were being annihilated, but they failed to act. Almost a year and a half later Henry Morgenthau, Jr., Secretary of the Treasury, and his courageous assistant, John Pehle, threatened to expose the policy of our government and submitted a scathing report to President Roosevelt. Only then did the President, on January 22, 1944, create the War Refugee Board to save the remaining Jews of Europe. During the preceding eighteen months, over two million Jews had been murdered. In 1944 and 1945, however, Ira Hirschmann, representing director Pehle

. . . survivor, with photograph of family members killed at Babi Yar

and his colleagues on the War Refugee Board, used many private as well as diplomatic channels to rescue significant numbers of Jews still alive in Europe.

During the years of abandonment and deportations, Vladka told me, the young people in the ghettos played a very important role. "They were the *soul* of the ghetto," she said. "They were really the avant garde of everything which happened in defense of human dignity. They were youth who didn't live by bread alone—although in the ghetto there was not too much bread. Even before the war, they were youth who lived with certain ideals, with certain beliefs. And this sustained them during the ghetto time—the horrible time—and gave them the strength to have a little bit of vision, even then, to be able to raise themselves up above the murderous pit . . . even, I would say, above the smoke of the crematories. They were the ones organizing cultural events; they were the ones organizing choirs in the ghettos, plays in the ghettos—young people! What young people! They kept the soul alive as long as people were alive." Youth in the Vilna Ghetto, for example, would get together in the evening (since deportations occurred during the day) and put on a new play, recite a new poem, or perform a new musical composition or song. "To be human beings to the end was thanks to the young people who would not give in," Vladka reflected. "And so young people can play a very important role in history in the most difficult times *if* they really have *beliefs*—if they don't live by bread alone."

Bennett Aaron, President, FJA (Philadelphia), addressing survivors

Ed Gastfriend at the candlelighting ceremony for the Six Million

Near the end of the Memorial Service, Ed Gastfriend, a survivor of Buchenwald, lit the last of the six candles of the *Yizkor* (memorial) lamp, each candle representing one million Jews who perished during the Holocaust. Remember, Mark, how impossible the number seemed when I told you that six million Jews had been killed? "The tragedy is *so big*," said Roman Kent, another survivor, "that it's losing its meaning as a tragedy, because you can't comprehend it. You can have *a bond* with one person, with two people, but you *cannot* with six million. This is one of the reasons why the tragedy is so great: It cannot be comprehended."

During the singing of *"El Molei Rachamim"* ("O God, Full of Compassion"), the

Marion Wilen, chairperson, Memorial Committee; Isaac Horowitz singing "El Molei Rachamim"

traditional Jewish prayer for the souls of the dead, Leo Korona proudly held a Torah that had been smuggled out of Czechoslovakia during the war. He carried this "Holocaust Torah," with its plaque commemorating the six million Jews, during the entire length of the "Road to Freedom" procession to Independence Mall. He died just a few months after the Gathering, at age 74. "God doesn't owe me anything," he told his wife on the day before he died. "I've had a wonderful life in the United States. It's forty years after the war—how many people made it? I'm a very lucky man."

Gary, their only child, never knew about his father's earlier life until, on the eve of Gary's bar mitzvah, Leo broke down in tears and began to talk. He told him that his first wife and their two children had died at Auschwitz, his little son murdered in front of his eyes after Leo had been discovered hiding him. Leo himself survived five more camps before his liberation by American troops at Mauthausen on May 5, 1945. "He was so thankful to the Americans," Gary told me. "When they arrived, the Nazis just dropped everything and ran. 'My life is miracles,' he would say."

Originally from Sosnowiec, Poland, Leo came to the United States in 1947 from a displaced persons (DP) camp in Germany. In 1950 he married Ilse Schoenmann

Leo Korona, survivor, with Holocaust Torah

Bina Landau, survivor, singing the partisans' hymn

of Vienna, also a survivor, and devoted his life to Jewish causes. He couldn't get to the Jerusalem or Washington Gatherings in 1981 and 1983 but was thrilled at the opportunity that Philadelphia presented in 1985. He met a number of people he hadn't seen for years. "It was my Dad's final chapter," said Gary.

The Torah that survived the Holocaust, resting in its ark at the synagogue where Leo served as president, evokes special memories for Gary. "My father thought that the rabbi should carry the Torah during the procession to Independence Hall," Gary recalled. "But the rabbi said, 'No, Leo, you're the survivor. The honor belongs to you.'" Gary has succeeded his father as chairperson of the annual Holocaust Weekend of Remembrance at the synagogue. "I'll be carrying the Torah," he said.

At the head of the procession to Independence Mall that Sunday afternoon were three grandchildren of survivors carrying a torch brought from Israel and lit from the flame of the *Yizkor* lamp by Benjamin Meed, survivor of the Warsaw Ghetto and President of the American Gathering. During the transfer of the torch, Bina Landau, a survivor from Radom, Poland, sang the closing hymn, *"Zog Nit Keyn Mol"* ("Never Say"), written by Hirsh Glik in Vilna upon hearing of the Warsaw Ghetto Uprising. So intense was her rendition, so electrifying the call to courage, and so manifest the message—its marching tempo compelling all to rise, singing—that only halfway through did I realize they were not singing in English. Later I learned that Glik's song is in Yiddish and set to a Russian melody. During the war it spread rapidly among the ghettos, forests, and concentration camps, inspiring Jews everywhere:

> Never say you've come to the end of the way,
> Though leaden skies block out the light of day.

This was the "partisans' hymn," the battle hymn of the Jewish resistance fighters, promising from out of the night:

> The hour we long for will surely appear—
> Our steps will thunder with the words: We are here!

Recently Bina told me that she is no longer well enough to sing, a condition that is hard for her to accept because music has been her life since childhood. As a little child she sang on the stage, and at the age of sixteen she was singing and performing, organizing concerts and plays in the Radom ghetto during its first weeks in the spring of 1941. And in the concentration camps—first Majdanek, then Plaszow, Auschwitz, and Bergen-Belsen—the voice of this slight teenager from Poland (she is only four feet, eleven inches tall) saved her life. She was instantly favored by fellow prisoners, who guarded her talent. Inmates with influence did whatever they could to keep Bina assigned to indoor jobs that exploited her clerical skills and fluency in both German and Polish. Thus spared the harsh outdoor labor, she found the energy to give spiritual strength in song to her suffering companions late at night in the barracks.

The year after liberation, Bina married a survivor from Bedzin, Marion Landau. Together they immigrated to the United States, arriving in New York Harbor aboard the *Marine Flasher*, a troop transport ship, on May 21, 1946. Bina and her husband came immediately to Philadelphia, where Marion became a successful businessman. Meanwhile, Bina attended and eventually graduated from Settlement Music School, beginning her professional singing career in 1952. For more than thirty years Bina sang in Yiddish and eight other languages on stages all over the world—Brazil, Canada, France, Mexico, and Israel, as well as in cities all over the United States— but she has never returned to Poland, where her two sisters and brother were killed by the Nazis. Today, weakened and confined to a wheelchair, Bina accepts no more singing engagements. "I sing only in my mind now," she says.

The procession to Independence Mall

Bearing signs of "Cities of Remembrance"

Volunteer, the procession to Independence Mall

First came the torchbearers, then children and volunteers bearing signs of European cities and towns where survivors once lived, then the survivors themselves with their children, followed by the general public, in the procession along the fourteen-block route to Independence Mall. It was a journey in stark contrast to the death marches that many of these same survivors endured forty years earlier. In the last months of the war, the Nazis evacuated Auschwitz and other camps, and, in the dead of winter, forced starving, exhausted, beaten, and ill-clad prisoners to go miles on foot away from the advancing Allied forces. All throughout the war years, many of those in the procession on Sunday had been slave laborers who marched every day in and out of the ghettos, or from the concentration camps to work sites, herded through the streets in full view of the local citizens.

Now the destination of the marchers, joined by civic and religious leaders in a public display of solidarity, was the heart and birthplace of America's freedom: Independence Hall and the Liberty Bell, which to the survivors symbolized liberation and the gift of new life in the United States. And what deep appreciation these survivors felt and continue to feel, forty years later, toward the American soldiers who liberated them from the horrors of Dachau, Nordhausen, Buchenwald, Flossenburg, Mauthausen, and other concentration camps, and from their subsidiaries, such as Wöbbelin and Ebensee. Several thousand of the estimated 300,000 Jews who survived the camps were paying tribute to those soldiers that afternoon. Over 70,000 survivors immigrated to the United States in the five years immediately following liberation, more than to any other nation except Israel. But an even greater number of survivors were saved from the inferno of Auschwitz *before* liberation by one man of uncompromising integrity and dedication: Raoul Wallenberg.

Here, Justine and Mark, is a hero truly worthy of your attention as you shape your image of what it means to be a great human being. Do you remember asking me, Mark, why, if so many people were being killed over such a long period of time, nobody did anything about it? The truth is that some who had the most power did the least, and some who had the least power did the most, although in all cases it was not nearly enough. Raoul Wallenberg, a thirty-two-year-old Swedish diplomat in Budapest, had some power, and by doing all he could with it, often at great risk to his own life, he succeeded in rescuing over 70,000 Hungarian Jews from certain death in the gas chambers of Auschwitz. Outwitting the Nazis again and again, he forged passports that guaranteed for Jews the protection of the Swedish government and established an international network of "safe houses" that the Nazis were legally barred from entering. He created nurseries, soup kitchens, and hospitals staffed by hundreds of Jews and was often seen personally administering food and care to those in need. Supported by funds issued through the U.S. War Refugee Board, 90 percent of it raised through private contributions, Raoul Wallenberg showed the world what could have been done much sooner had its leaders possessed the moral and political will to attempt it. After seven months of life-saving work, this man of great courage and compassion was arrested by the Russians as a suspected American spy on January 17, 1945. It is not known to this day whether this "righteous Gentile" and "hero of the Holocaust" is still alive somewhere in the Soviet Union. Efforts to find out where he is and to achieve his release continue, though hope grows dimmer with each passing year. Meanwhile, he remains for all of us a decent, indeed noble, human being, a model of political power in the service of humanity. On the medal given to his surviving family by Yad Vashem (the Martyrs' and Heroes' Remembrance Authority, in Jerusalem) is a saying from the Talmud that challenges us today as we remember the example of Raoul Wallenberg: "Whoever saves a single soul, it is as if he had saved the whole world."

Preparing banner for the procession

Honoring Raoul Wallenberg and . . .

. . . appealing for his release

"Cities of Remembrance" at Independence Hall

The procession culminated at Independence Hall with the formal opening event of the Gathering. Rabbi Boruch Leizerowski, a survivor of the Lodz ghetto, offered a brief prayer, followed by the remarks of John Cardinal Krol, Archbishop of Philadelphia. Benjamin Meed then spoke, facing the Liberty Bell housed several hundred feet across the mall. "Never shall we forget that American soldiers offered the ultimate sacrifice to defeat Nazism," he said. But he and other speakers looked at more recent events and saw in them ominous tokens of forgetfulness. Ten days earlier, the White House had announced that the President of the United States and Chancellor Kohl of West Germany were going to commemorate the end of World War II and the healing of wounds between the two countries by placing wreaths on the burial grounds of a military cemetery in Bitburg, a small town in West Germany near the border of Luxembourg. The event was to take place on May 5, two weeks after the Gathering. The symbolism became savagely distorted, however, when it was revealed soon after the announcement that about fifty men and officers of the *Waffen*-SS were buried in Bitburg alongside soldiers of the regular German army. (It was units of these *Waffen* ["armed"]-SS who carried out and recruited collaborators for the mass killing of Jews as each city or town fell to the Germans. After mid-1940, some regiments of the *Waffen*-SS included members of the *Totenkopfverbände,* or "Death's-Head units," SS who had served as armed guards in the concentration camps.) Although there was time to choose another site for the ceremony, President Reagan instead announced as an afterthought on

Rabbi Leizerowski at the opening ceremonies, Independence Hall

April 19, the eve of the Gathering, that he would lay a wreath at Bergen-Belsen, too. Bitburg would not be cancelled. As he had said earlier, those buried there were "victims [of Nazism], just as surely as the victims in the concentration camps."

"How many of those buried at Bitburg were on duty at Dachau or Buchenwald?" asked Menachem Rosensaft, founding chairman of the International Network of Children of Jewish Holocaust Survivors, in his speech that afternoon. "I stand here as the son of two survivors of Auschwitz and Bergen-Belsen, whose father, Josef Rosensaft, is no longer alive to speak out." Menachem was born in Bergen-Belsen after liberation, when the site had been converted into a DP camp. "The image— the photograph—of the President of the United States laying a wreath in the name of the United States at a cemetery where SS men are buried is certain to be exploited by revisionist historians, neo-Nazis, and their assorted sympathizers as proof that

Survivors inside Liberty Bell Pavilion, Independence Mall

the perpetrators of the Holocaust have been forgiven and that it is now all right to forget." In response to wide criticism of his intended actions by both Jews and non-Jews, the President had succeeded only in manufacturing, in Menachem Rosensaft's words, "an obscene package-deal of Bitburg and Bergen-Belsen," and in further obscuring the original issue, which was, as Elie Wiesel had clarified earlier, "not politics, but good and evil."

After six symbolic rings of the tower bell of Independence Hall and the sounding of the shofar—the sacred ram's horn blown in synagogues at Rosh Hashanah and Yom Kippur—survivors completed their mile-long procession by filing slowly into the pavilion that houses the Liberty Bell. Whereas Bitburg had already threatened to become a symbol of historical amnesia and false reconciliation, Philadelphia that afternoon became the setting for a simple act of sincere remembrance. One by one, survivors placed carnations in the wicker baskets beneath the Liberty Bell, expressing in this way their appreciation of the freedom they have enjoyed in America.

The Ross family with flowers, outside Liberty Bell Pavilion

The building housing the Liberty Bell was crowded with survivors, so I decided to remain outside until later, photographing those standing in line and others strolling on the green between that building and Independence Hall. Suddenly I saw Gabe Ross, who had been a co-worker of mine back in the seventies. We were surprised to see each other. I had not known that he is the child of survivors.

Gabe's parents had escaped to the Soviet sector of Poland after the German occupation of the western part in 1939. Because they refused to become Soviet citizens, however, they were considered "capitalists," or "potential spies," and were thus sent to Siberia. They met in a labor camp in 1940. After the German invasion of the Soviet Union in June 1941, amnesty was declared for Polish citizens, and Gabe's parents decided to make their way to the Chinese border, wishing to stay as far away from Europe as possible. Gabe was born on January 24, 1943, in Kazakhstan, a Russian state bordering on Outer Mongolia and China. The family returned to Poland after the war, then escaped to the West, reaching the United States in 1950.

Couple at Independence Mall

Dinah Stern Tausig, Milford (Connecticut), with flower

I met Dinah Stern Tausig in front of the speakers' platform at Independence Hall. Her husband, Ted, was doing volunteer work for the British Embassy in Vienna when Hitler took over Austria in March 1938. Ted had filled out all the necessary papers for a visa to England and had just left the post office when he was arrested by the Gestapo (security police of the SS). He and a number of other Jews were later herded into a makeshift detention center in the stable of a local riding academy. When brought before a committee ten days later, he was able to promise that he would be out of the country within two weeks. Poor, but with a visa, he was saved by his connections with the British Embassy. Ted got to England, then to America in 1939, later that year meeting Dinah, a Jew who was born on New York's Lower East Side.

Ted died at age 72, two months before the Gathering. Dinah said that he would not have attended even had he been able, for he rarely spoke about his painful experience and family losses. His mother died of a heart attack—brought on by fear, Ted was convinced—shortly after her two sisters were deported to Auschwitz. Ted had been working hard as a leather craftsman for a handbag manufacturer in New York City and saving money to purchase his mother's passage to the United States. Since Ted's death, Dinah has become the chronicler of his story and the effect of his experiences on their entire family, consisting now of six grandchildren in addition to the two daughters and son he left behind.

It was only after their daughter, Etta, had survived the "children's action" in the ghetto in Kovno, capital city of Lithuania, that Rachel and Rafael Levin finally decided to risk smuggling her out of the ghetto. The risk of being caught was great, but keeping their only child in the ghetto had become even more dangerous. On March 27–28, 1944, the SS, in a brutal house-to-house search, rounded up virtually all of the several thousand children under age thirteen still remaining in the ghetto. Torn from their parents, the children were driven by the truckload to a site outside the ghetto, where they were murdered. Etta was among the very few not discovered in the roundup. She was well hidden and, at the age of five, well tutored in survival skills. "I remember the boots climbing up the stairs," she said. "I was hidden in the space directly below, afraid even to breathe." Ever since the slaughter two years earlier of over 9,000 Jews—almost half of them children—on one day in the fall of 1942, she had been learning to be unnaturally quiet and to accept not being allowed to go outside to play. Somehow she retained a kind of childhood in her isolated daytime world beneath the table where she hid, drew pictures, daydreamed, and hated the Nazis, who were often the subject of her "getting even" pictures.

Her parents, meanwhile, had been preparing her for the day when she would have to live with strangers, until the family could be reunited. That day came right after the March massacre. A priest involved in underground rescue operations had found her a place with a Catholic family. Etta remembers never moving or making a sound, while she lay bunched up in a potato sack for what seemed an endless time as her mother smuggled her out of the ghetto in her arms. Four months later, the ghetto was liquidated. The men were sent to Dachau and its subsidiary camps in Germany, and the women to Stutthof, the renamed fishermen's village of Sztutowo, near Gdansk (Danzig). During the first transport by cattle car out of Kovno, her parents had agreed that one of them would try to escape. In transit, Rafael was helped up to a small gap in the roof of the cattle car. He struggled through, jumped to safety, and escaped into the woods. For weeks he hid in the fields, barns, and haystacks of Lithuanian farmers in the region, at last finding one Gentile farmer who sheltered and fed him until after the Russians had occupied Kovno. He returned to the city in September and was reunited with his daughter.

So cautious had Etta become during the six intervening months that when her father appeared at the home with a coloring book for her, and asked her gently, "Do you remember me?"—she would not respond. Only after he took her outside for a walk, and they were totally alone, did she acknowledge him. Her mother survived Stutthof and was reunited with them several months afterward.

Etta never spoke publicly about her childhood experiences until 1983 at a Holocaust conference at Ursinus College. She spoke out then to counter revisionist historians, who seek to deny the extent, or even the fact, of the Holocaust. "It's like a knife in the back," she says of their efforts to distort the truth. After her speech at the conference, a man approached. He had been one of the American soldiers who liberated Dachau and its 30,000 survivors, including 2,500 Jews, mostly from Lithuania. "I know it happened," he told her. "I was there."

Etta Levin Hecht, child survivor of Kovno

Libbie Braverman with flower, late afternoon on the Mall

Libbie Braverman, a writer and lecturer on the teaching of Jewish history, is currently writing her memoirs of forty years devoted to Jewish education in Cleveland, Ohio. She came to the Gathering even though she is not a survivor and lost no relatives during the Holocaust. This teacher, now in her seventies, believes that one can never learn enough about this most tragic period in Jewish history. It was late in the afternoon, almost dusk, when I made this photograph of Libbie on my way back from the Liberty Bell pavilion.

Flowers at the base of the Liberty Bell, end of day

Survivors' Village, Civic Center

Kurt Adler, Survivors' Village

The next day the locus of activity shifted to the Civic Center, "Survivors' Village" in particular, where I met Kurt Adler. On the night of November 9, 1938, Kurt was forced from his home in Frankfurt-am-Main together with an estimated 30,000 other Jews throughout Germany and Austria, all of whom were rounded up and sent to concentration camps. That night and the next day, hundreds of Jewish shops, homes, and synagogues were looted and burned—many of them completely destroyed. So much broken glass was produced by this widespread destruction of Jewish property that the Nazis referred to that night as *Kristallnacht*, "Night of the Broken Glass." It was a clear sign of what was yet to come for the Jews under Hitler. A week later, all Jewish children were expelled from German schools, the climax of the harassment and ridicule that they had been suffering in German classrooms since 1933.

TABLE MAP OF
SURVIVORS' VILLAGE

Detail, information area, Survivors' Village

Most of the Jews sent to concentration camps as part of the *Kristallnacht* terror were released within a few months, but not before an estimated 1,000 had been murdered. Those released had to promise to leave Germany within a week. Kurt Adler was one of those not released, but early in 1940 he and two other inmates of Buchenwald devised an escape plan. While working with the burial unit, the three arranged through a fourth person to be hidden in wooden coffins that were to be taken out of camp that night for burial. Once they were a good distance from the gate, they got out of the coffins, overcame and killed the surprised Nazi officer and his driver, and fled into the forest. Aided by resistance forces, Kurt reached England later that year and shortly thereafter immigrated to the United States.

The Survivors' Village area of the Civic Center consisted of dozens of tables, each with a small metal stand bearing a namecard of a city or town in Europe with sizable pre-war Jewish populations. The idea, of course, was that survivors

Interviews and discussion: survivors searching for survivors

Bulletin board, Survivors' Village

might be thus aided in their search for relatives and friends from those places, or from the numerous villages surrounding them. For many survivors who had lost absolutely everyone, even a total stranger would have been a remarkable and welcomed find. In Poland, for example, more than 4,000 Jewish communities were completely annihilated by the Nazis. Of the estimated 3,300,000 Jews alive in Poland at the time of the German invasion in September 1939, only 300,000—10 percent—were still alive in May 1945. Even then, though the war had ended, anti-Semitism had not, and historians have documented that an estimated 1,000 additional Jews were murdered in pogroms and other acts of violence as they returned from the concentration camps to their Polish hometowns and cities during the next two years.

These shattering statistics gave context to the wandering and seaching that continued all through the weekend in Survivors' Village. Again and again I was

Symcha Rusinek, survivor

moved by the pride and perseverance of survivors like Symcha Rusinek, of Maplewood, New Jersey, who lost both parents, his only sister, and every one of his other relatives from Bedzin—a town in southern Poland less than a hundred miles from Auschwitz—but hadn't lost his will to live or his unyielding hope. "I wore the crown cap," he told me, "so that more people would notice where I was from—and maybe I'd find someone after all these years." He didn't.

More often than not, survivors and visitors overlooked the table signs and simply sat down at the nearest one to converse, have a snack, or enjoy a few minutes of rest. A survivor from Vilna might be talking to someone from Odessa at the Budapest table. It didn't matter. I was at all the tables, trying to document the many interactions taking place. The abundance of joy in Abraham Bayer's face as he hugged Siegi Izakson led me to believe at first that they were two survivors who probably had not seen each other for forty years. What I learned, however, is that Abraham, a native-born American, sees his friend Siegi, a Holocaust survivor, many times as they cross paths in their efforts to support the cause of Soviet Jews. "I would have that expression on my face if I hadn't seen him for *a day*!" Abraham said when I showed him the photograph I had taken. "I love him! And I'm glad he's alive. He's a witness and we're running out of them."

Brought up and educated in Warsaw, Siegi was a teenager on vacation with his mother in the Carpathian Mountains, visiting his grandparents in Sosnowiec, near Auschwitz, when war broke out in 1939. They couldn't return to Warsaw. Only after the war did he learn that all of his father's family had perished in the ghetto. "My father had five brothers and four sisters," he said. "I was the only Izakson left." Today his two sons—one a rabbi, the other a businessman—carry on the family name and heritage so nearly extinguished forty years ago. Siegi, President of the Houston Council of Jewish Holocaust Survivors, is a survivor of Gross Rosen, Groeditz, Faulbrük, Blechhammer, Auschwitz, and finally Niederorschel, a subcamp of Buchenwald. In March 1945 he escaped while on a death march from there to Buchenwald. After a few days of alternate walking and hiding, he posed as a Polish laborer and got work on a farm in a village near the city of Erfurt. He could see Buchenwald from the hill where he tended the cows, and after a week of gradually increasing artillery noise, American troops arrived in the village on their way toward the camp.

"If they had let me, I would have kissed each one of them!" he remembers. "Even after liberation, though, common sense told me not to reveal my true identity. Two or three days later I went back to Buchenwald, where I knew I would be safe." The first American troops arrived there on April 11, and still others were arriving on the day that Siegi returned. "Hardly any survivors had a dry eye when the battalions marched in with their flags." Many soldiers wept, too, but not for joy. "I saw Dante's Hell," Siegi recalls of that day. "Piles of corpses lying there dead of starvation, disease, exhaustion. I saw soldiers in tears." For twenty-five years afterward he could not respond to death or share his experiences. "Only when we were eventually able to talk about it and realize—We lived!—did the implications of survival finally hit us," he said. "If we had been *rational* about it, we would never have been able to begin a new life. It was because we blocked it out that we were able, unintentionally, to get on with new life." He has been speaking out ever since.

Though not a survivor, Siegi's friend, Abraham Bayer, is another kind of witness. He was born in New York City on April 19, 1932, eleven years—to the day—before the Warsaw Ghetto Uprising. "I remember the photographs in the *Forward* [popular Yiddish daily newspaper] of the burning Warsaw ghetto," he told me in his office at the National Jewish Community Relations Advisory Council (NJCRAC) in New York. "I remember them. They were smuggled out and published." Abraham was only eleven years old then, Mark, just as you are now, but he traces his commitment to remember and to implement the lessons of the Holocaust to those revelations. "Even though I wasn't in the concentration camps, I feel myself to be a witness because I was cognizant at that period. Now to me that's a responsibility. If I can remember a photograph of a synagogue or the ghetto burning, I'm a witness. Obviously I'm not a firsthand witness, like somebody who was there, but *I remember*." Abraham, Director of International Affairs for NJCRAC, is the only officer of the American Gathering who is not a Holocaust survivor.

Siegi and Abraham, Survivors' Village

Rabbi Avigdor, survivor

Rabbi Isaac Avigdor of Hartford, Connecticut, was born in Santz, Poland, a small town near Cracow. He was a young rabbi in the town of Boryslaw, Eastern Galicia, assisting his father, Rabbi Dr. Jacob Avigdor, at the time of the German *Blitzkrieg*. A survivor of the Mauthausen concentration camp, Isaac suffered nightmares for years and was also plagued by subconscious feelings of guilt that *he* had survived while so many others, including all but three of the sixty or so members of his extended family, had perished. It took twenty-five years, and much encouragement

Amy Small, volunteer

from his children before he could begin to put down on paper his experiences. Since then he has published two autobiographical accounts. "We are the last will and testament of those who were destroyed," he said.

I hadn't seen Amy Small for three years when I ran into her at the Gathering, where she was a volunteer. We had worked together as counselors fourteen years earlier—she remembers your birth, Justine!—but I hadn't known that many of her relatives died in the Holocaust. "My grandfather was here in the United States, but

Volunteers assisting survivors, National Computer Register

just about everybody else was over there," she told me, "over there" being Ciechanowiec, a small town in the Bialystok region of northeastern Poland. Late in the fall of 1942, more than 90 percent of the Jews of the town were deported to Auschwitz. "My great-grandmother used to write all the time, my uncle told me, but then suddenly there were no letters ever again."

Her grandfather knew everything about the family, Amy was told, so she bought tapes sometime in 1980 to record the conversations she meant to have with him. But before she got around to putting her plan into action, he died unexpectedly in 1981. Four years later, Amy was conducting interviews for the Gratz College Oral History Archive, taping the accounts of survivors—"Before it's too late," she said.

Many kinds of interviews took place that weekend. At long tables in an area adjacent to Survivors' Village, volunteers helped survivors enter their names, addresses, and other identifying information into the computers of the National Register of Jewish Holocaust Survivors. This is the quickest and most thorough way available for survivors to seek out family members and friends who might still be alive. It began in Jerusalem with the first World Gathering of Jewish Holocaust Survivors in the summer of 1981. At that time, several thousand survivors entered their biographical information into the computer bank, and hundreds were reunited. By 1983, the time of the first American Gathering in Washington, D.C., hundreds

Volunteers assisting survivors, National Computer Register

more had made contacts as the number of registrants swelled to more than 40,000. Now the figure has increased to more than 50,000 and is still growing. The second and third generations have been urged to enter their data as well, and it is hoped that eventually 100,000 names and biographical profiles will be registered, constituting an important repository of historical material extending well beyond the lives and dwindling numbers of the survivors themselves.

Group of students attending the Gathering

Journalist recording sentiments of students after testimony by survivors

Jack Zawid, from Vladimir-Volynskiy (near Kiev), telling students how he survived

Students with survivor, learning about the Holocaust

Sarah Kirsch (r.), sharing family photographs in Survivors' Village

Sarah Kirsch of Kalamazoo, Michigan, came to the Gathering in search of other relatives who might have survived as her parents did, hoping that they might share some of their experiences with her, as neither of her parents had been able to do. "For years I was very much at my wits' end wondering about my identity," Sarah said. Her mother, who had lost both parents in the Holocaust, died in 1978. "She really didn't talk about things the way she needed to," Sarah told me. Her father, too, is silent. He lost both parents as well as five sisters and brothers. A tailor, he survived Dachau by doing alterations on Nazi uniforms. Though Sarah found no relatives in Philadelphia, and no names in the computer, she did meet other children of survivors, sons and daughters of parents who won't, or simply can't, speak about what they experienced. So these children of survivors talked to one another, and for Sarah this proved to be the beginning of her personal healing.

Gertrude Rosenblat came from a large family, but only she and two cousins, one from each side of the family, survived the Holocaust. She was fourteen years old in 1941 when she was deported from the Radom Ghetto to Skarzysko-Kamienna, a slave-labor camp in Poland. For three years she worked in the ammunitions factory there. In 1944 she was transferred to a camp near Czestochowa, and soon afterward, in January 1945, she and several thousand fellow prisoners began a terrible death march westward, away from the fast-approaching Russians. After trudging pitifully through the snow for a mile or so, Gertrude and two others

Sarah's parents, Bronia Bergman and Morris Kirsch, of Lachova, Poland

decided to risk an escape attempt. They threw themselves into a ditch by the side of the road. Having successfully eluded notice, they then struggled through the fields in bitter cold, snow above their knees, leaning on each other for support, progressing slowly through the long night. Eventually they came to a farm. "We hid in the farmer's pig house," Gertrude said. "When he discovered us there in the morning, he was shocked. He asked if we were from a concentration camp. When we said 'Yes,' he told us to get out. We were scared, though, and wouldn't move." The farmer left abruptly, only to return shortly with another man who turned out to be from one of the other labor camps in the area. He told them that they were free: The Red Army had arrived in Czestochowa on the very day their death march had begun.

Gertrude and her companions made their way back to the city, free for the first

Gertrude Rosenblat (r.), with two other survivors from New Orleans

time in five years. As displaced persons, they would struggle to begin life over again—whatever of it they still possessed, or could find, or could create out of almost nothing, as in Gertrude's case when she discovered that both her parents and all seven of her older brothers and sisters had been murdered.

She returned to Radom briefly, then married Ralph Rosenblat in 1946. Later that same year, in the DP camp in Stuttgart, their daughter Ruth was born. Henry, their second child, was born in 1950, two years after they arrived in the U.S. and moved to New Orleans to live near some of Ralph's relatives. "My children brought me back to life," she said. But every night she goes to sleep with the names of her four brothers and three sisters on her lips. "I say 'Goodnight' to them, and then I say, 'Mommy and Daddy, wherever you are, watch over me.'"

Months after our conversation, I am looking at the photograph of Gertrude that I took in Survivors' Village. I look at the face of this sixty-year-old woman sitting at a table with her two friends. She and her husband have two grown children now, and four grandchildren. And their business, Ralph's Kosher Meat and Delicatessen, is still thriving after thirty-five years. I look at her hand just touching the compact, open on the table, next to a tube of lipstick. Everything looks perfectly . . . ordinary. She could be my aunt, I think. And this could be any other occasion but a gathering of Holocaust survivors. Then I take out my notes from our conversation and recite the litany of names she repeats every night before falling asleep: "Abush, Gabriel, Shama, Rokhl, Bache, Chana, Ayzik . . ."

Edith Greifinger Millman, survivor of Warsaw Ghetto

I first met Edith Millman six years ago through my lifelong friend and "Jewish mother," Nora Levin, who went to school with my mother. Because Edith speaks both German and Polish, she found it possible, after escaping from the Warsaw Ghetto, to pass as an Aryan during the war years. Like all survivors passing as Aryans, she lived in constant fear of being "discovered," as indeed she was, more than once. Do you remember my telling you, Justine, about the seventeen-year-old girl whose former schoolmate from eighth grade recognized her one day on the street and immediately reported her to the Gestapo? It was Edith who was betrayed. In a subsequent narrow escape, she glanced back while fleeing from her place of work only to witness her boyfriend being fatally shot point-blank in the head, seconds after spotting the approaching Gestapo officers and shouting for her to run.

She cannot recount this story, nor the many other scenes of violence she witnessed in those days, without tears welling in her eyes. Yet she continues to bear witness, speaking to adult groups and students in high schools and colleges in the Philadelphia area. One memorable evening several years ago, she shared her experiences with a class I was teaching locally for Wilmington College. Each of us came away a changed person. Both of Edith's parents also survived—her mother after escaping the ghetto as an Aryan, her father by hiding in various places. A prostitute saved his life during one gap between hiding places, harboring him for several weeks until he found other quarters. Another time Edith hid him in her own small room, which was connected by French doors to the rest of the apartment occupied by an unsuspecting German family. When Edith went out to work, her father had to hide under the bed for the entire time, not making a sound.

Within the past few years, both her parents have died. She is now working on a translation of her mother's memoirs.

Much of one entire day at the Civic Center was spent on reports of the behavior of the Allies—America in particular—during the Holocaust. The material was presented by researchers, witnesses, and other authorities on the subject. One of the most passionate accounts of the Free World's abandonment of the Jews was delivered by Jan Karski. A liaison officer between the Polish Government-in-Exile in London and the Polish Underground, Karski was smuggled into the Warsaw Ghetto twice in the fall of 1942. He saw with his own eyes what he called, in *Story of a Secret State* (1944), "a new world, utterly unlike anything that had been imagined. . . . Everywhere there was hunger, the atrocious stench of decomposing bodies, the pitiful moans of dying children." Five weeks later he reported his experience to the leaders of the Free World and urged them to act to save the Jews. He also reported his daring entry into the Belzec death camp where, disguised as an Estonian guard, he witnessed Jews being packed into boxcars. The floors of the cars had been covered with quicklime to achieve their agonizing deaths by suffocation after the slow combustion of their sweating bodies in contact with the thick white powder. In this way the murder of Jews could continue, even when the gas chambers were not functioning properly or when the overflow of Jews exceeded the operating capacity—15,000 victims per day.

Karski delivered this report in person to President Roosevelt, as well as to members of the British Parliament and other leaders among the Allies, but they did not take action in response. In his speech that day at the Gathering, it seemed as if it were 1942 again and Karski was pleading with *us* to do something. And indeed he *was* pleading with us: Never to forget, never to allow such conditions to prevail again, never to become complacent in the face of human misery, never to think that the impossibly evil may not in fact be possible and actually happening—and never to think that we ourselves might not be capable of it! Karski nearly collapsed after his speech, and only reluctantly did he put up with a brief medical evaluation as he sat down in the front row of the audience, shaking and sweating, brushing off all shows of concern that he might need fresh air, help, something.

"I know history," wrote Jan Karski, now Professor Emeritus of Slavic Studies at Georgetown University. "I have learned a great deal about the evolution of nations, political systems, social doctrines, methods of conquest, persecution, and extermination, and I know, too, that never in the history of mankind, never anywhere in the realm of human relations, did anything occur to compare with what was inflicted on the Jewish population of Poland."

Jan Karski, assisted by Benjamin Meed after testifying at the Civic Center

Leon Bass, liberator, testifying at the Civic Center

"When I walked through the gates of the camp, I saw these people who looked like the 'walking dead,'" Leon Bass told me, recounting his experience as a corporal in the 183rd Engineer Combat Battalion, which participated in the liberation of Buchenwald in April 1945. "They just came tumbling forward, some of them making almost animal sounds—skin and bones, dressed in pajama-type uniforms with their heads shaved . . . skeletons with deep-set eyes. I looked at these people, and I couldn't believe what I was seeing. I didn't know what to do. I had just turned twenty, and I didn't know what to do."

For twenty-five years Leon Bass never talked about the horror he had seen. Then one day in the fall of 1970, as he was making his daily rounds as principal of Benjamin Franklin High School—an all male, mostly Black school in North Philadelphia—he glanced into a room and saw students laughing and talking among themselves, ignoring a woman who was standing in front of the class and trying to communicate with them. "I walked into the classroom and sat down," he recalled. "I began to gather that this woman was a survivor trying to tell her story. 'Listen!' I said to the kids. 'This woman has something to say, and it's true— I was there.'" Only at that point was there silence. "And of course as soon as they started hearing and really listening for a few minutes—then she had captured them. They listened, then asked questions. She showed them the number tattooed on her arm, and when she was finished they thanked her—and quietly left the room. And then she came to me with tears in her eyes, thanking me for becoming involved."

That day, at the age of forty-five, Leon Bass connected his pain as a Black soldier with the pain of that Jewish survivor. "When I went into the army, I was sent one way, and the White fellows were sent another way. Uncle Sam segregated me. He put me in a Black unit, telling me that I was not good enough, that I must be

**Cpl. Bass (arrow) at Buchenwald, April 1945
(Photo: Sgt. William A. Scott)**

relegated to this kind of status. And I resented it." The prejudice he had known as a child "up North" in Philadelphia—segregated seating in movie theaters, swimming pools he wasn't allowed to swim in—became much worse in the military. "I went to a fountain to drink some water in Macon, Georgia, where I was stationed at Camp Wheeler, and before I could drink, one of my Black friends grabbed me and said, 'Hey, Don't drink there!' And I looked up and saw the sign. It said: 'White.' . . . I got on a bus in Grenada, Mississippi. I walked to the back . . . but there were no seats—Black folks occupied them all. So I turned around and I looked. There were empty seats up front, but I had to stand for a hundred miles."

He was shipped overseas to fight Hitler and the Nazis. "But inside me, as an eighteen-year-old, I kept feeling this pain. Now this is the pain I took with me through Germany, through Luxembourg, through the Battle of the Bulge—through all that death and dying—and through which I kept saying to myself, 'Leon, what in the heck are you doing here? You're risking your life—for what? You can't get a drink of water, you can't ride a bus, you can't get food to eat—and yet you're standing out here with the possibility of *dying* fighting for some rights that belong to somebody else . . .

"I took this through Germany, and then I went into Buchenwald. . . . You could see the dead stacked up in piles, waiting their turn to go into the crematorium. And I looked in the crematorium, into the oven, and saw the charred remains of bodies. I saw the torture chamber with blood on the floor and on the slab, and the instruments still there, of torture. I saw the clothing of children stacked up in neat piles. I saw the parts of the human anatomy that they put in formaldehyde in jars and labeled. . . ."

He felt numb, then nauseated. He left the last building where the ovens were, and stood by the gate, waiting for the others to come out.

"It was then I realized that I could not have a narrow view of things," he said. "I had to realize that human suffering is universal. It's not just relegated to me and mine. And I made connections. People suffer, human beings suffer, and if I can connect my pain with your pain, it makes sense. That's why, when that survivor was trying to talk in the classroom, I made connections. Somehow we had to reach out to each other. And I felt, well, maybe this is the way I can do it. So I've been doing it ever since."

Leon, a Quaker, is co-chairperson of the board of Philadelphia's Interfaith Council on the Holocaust, founded in 1977 to develop ways to educate the public on the Holocaust, particularly through school curricula and through yearly symposia and special projects. He speaks frequently about his experiences as a liberator and, in fact, spoke for the American delegation of liberators during their first international conference, held in Washington, D.C., in 1982. "My mission is to talk about the past only insomuch as it's going to help me to make today better—and our future, for our kids. I want to make a difference now, and I want tomorrow to be better. And even if I'm not here, I want it to be better for our grandchildren. Some people say, 'Oh, it could never happen in this country.' I'm sorry," Leon said, "but I would not put my freedom up to a public referendum. I don't feel that secure, even in America. There's no balm in Gilead, I don't think—not yet. I think there's a lot to be done."

The little girl and her father in the photograph at right are looking at photos that are part of a large collection, "The Liberators," displayed at the Gathering by the Center for Holocaust Studies, Documentation and Research, founded in Brooklyn in 1974. The Center exists to provide a permanent record of photographs and oral testimony from American soldiers who liberated concentration camp inmates and helped in their relief and rehabilitation.

Documentary photographs and testimony by American liberators

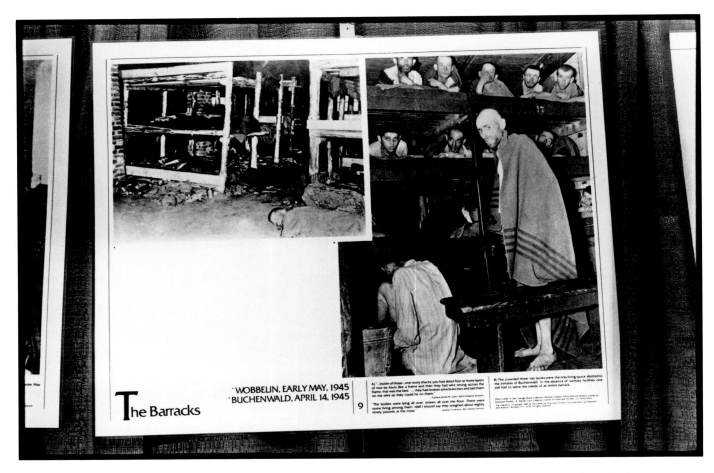

The barracks: Wöbbelin and Buchenwald, 1945 (from "The Liberators," Center for Holocaust Studies [Brooklyn])

The text for the image in the upper left corner ("Wöbbelin, Early May, 1945") reads as follows: "'... inside of those ... one-story shacks, you had about four or more layers of two-by-fours ... like a frame and then they had wire strung across the frame, that was the bed. ... they had broken pine branches and laid them on the wire so they could lie down on them.' (General James A. Gavin, 82nd Airborne Division)." And: "'The bodies were lying all over, strewn all over the floor. ... There were some living among them. Well, I should say they weighed about eighty, ninety pounds at the most.' (Nathan Putterman, 8th Infantry Division)."

The photograph to its right carries the following caption: "The crowded three-tier bunks were the only living space allotted to the inmates of Buchenwald. In the absence of sanitary facilities, one pail had to serve the needs of an entire barrack."

I had already met Bob Weil and heard some of his unusual story before the day I made this photograph outside the Civic Center. On *Kristallnacht* he had been forced from his home in Karlsruhe, Germany, and imprisoned in the concentration camp at Dachau. Before his arrest, however, he had applied for immigration to the United States under the French quota—he had been born in Metz, a city in the Alsace-Lorraine area of France, and U.S. visas are granted based on country of birth, not citizenship. When he was released from Dachau a few months later at the insistence of the French consul in Karlsruhe, he found the visa waiting for him at

"He liberated my father! He liberated my father!"

home; thus, within the same month as his release—February 1939—he was on a ship to the United States with his French visa and German passport.

"Jews born in Germany had little chance of getting to America at that time," he said. "There was something like an eight-year waiting list, so if I had been born in Germany and hence eligible for only a German visa, I would probably have ended up one of the six million. Luckily, instead of being number 20,000 or so in line for a German visa, I was number 94 for a French one—and out of the country within days."

Once safely in the United States, he applied for American citizenship papers in 1939, joined the U.S. Army in 1941, went overseas in 1943, and participated with the U.S. 8th Infantry Division in the liberation of the Nazi death camps in 1945. Why had he returned to Europe after escaping the Holocaust? "I felt so grateful to this country for giving me a second chance of life," he said, "that I wanted to go back to fight the Nazis as an American Jew."

As I was leaving the Civic Center on the afternoon of the last day of the Gathering, I heard a shout: It was Bob, waving me over as he was being hugged and kissed by an overjoyed woman. "He liberated my father! He liberated my father!" she exclaimed as I approached.

The woman was Frances Rogala, who had come to his assistance two days earlier, at the Memorial Service. It had been a hot day, and she noticed in the crowd a man who was about to faint. She moved quickly, reaching him just in time to catch him as he collapsed. She undid his collar and, with some help, got him to a clear space. Within minutes, Bob Weil had recovered. He and his wife were still thanking Frances profusely as she left. When they ran into each other again, two days later, she asked how he was feeling. "Fine, since you *liberated* me the other day!" he answered, jokingly. As they continued talking, Frances discovered that Bob himself actually had been a liberator—of Wöbbelin, the concentration camp where her father had been an inmate.

Frances was born in 1953 and thus never knew her brother and sister who had died years before in the Holocaust. Her mother and father had been living in Lask, a small town near Lodz in central Poland. In 1942 their two children were taken from them and murdered by the Nazis, a truth her father had refused to believe until, all too soon, the proof was forced upon him. The remaining Jews of Lask and other surrounding towns and villages had been sent to the Lodz Ghetto, where Frances's father was assigned to the work unit sorting clothes for redistribution as they came in from the ghetto and outlying killing sites. One day he recognized his little daughter's dress and his son's knickers among the piles of clothes he was sorting. He was never the same afterward and has always found it difficult to talk to Frances about those days. Nor did he want to come to the Gathering.

"I put my father's name in the computer register, hoping to find some relative who might have survived," Frances said, "someone—anyone—I could bring back as a gift to my father. But the only name that came up was my own."

Bob Weil turned out to be the gift that she could bring back to her father: a liberator whom she herself had been able to touch and thank. Returning home to Silver Spring, Maryland, Frances announced to her father: "Daddy, I did find someone! Someone who liberated you in Wöbbelin—and I gave him a big kiss for you!"

Deep was the gratitude expressed all weekend long to the American liberators. Nothing, however, could equal the depth of the pain and loss that survivors and their children continue to feel. And nothing that weekend more thoroughly documented the political and military machinery that inflicted this suffering and death upon the Jews than Arthur Cohn's documentary film, *The Final Solution,* which had its world premiere Sunday evening of the Gathering. The title echoes the verbal camouflage used by Reichsmarschall Hermann Goering to refer to the planned *physical annihilation* of all of Europe's Jews. Goering employed this euphemism in a written directive to Reinhard Heydrich, Head of the SD (Security Service), dated July 31, 1941, giving Heydrich absolute power "for the implementation of the desired final solution [*Endlösung*] of the Jewish question."

While viewing this film in the packed auditorium of Convention Hall, I took some photos of scenes of the concentration camps and the Warsaw Ghetto, shown

in the bottom row of photographs on the next several pages. The top row are photographs I took during the course of the weekend. The silence of the audience during the showing of this remarkable film was pierced several times by the pained shouts of survivors, who may have recognized themselves or someone they knew in the newsreels and other documentary footage, some of which had never before been shown.

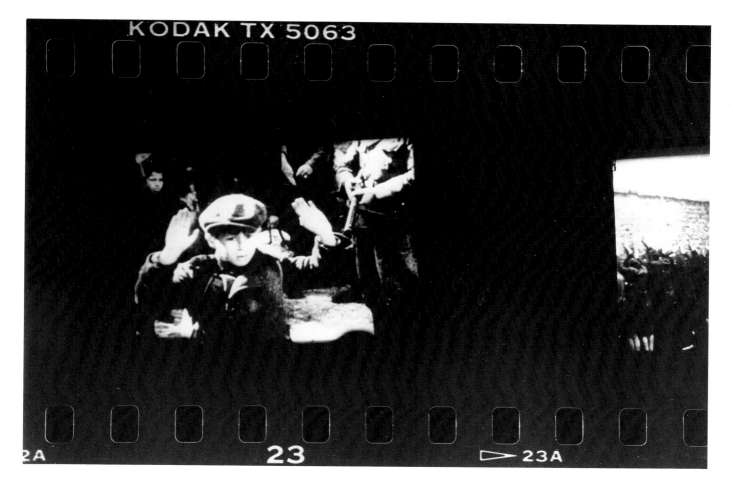

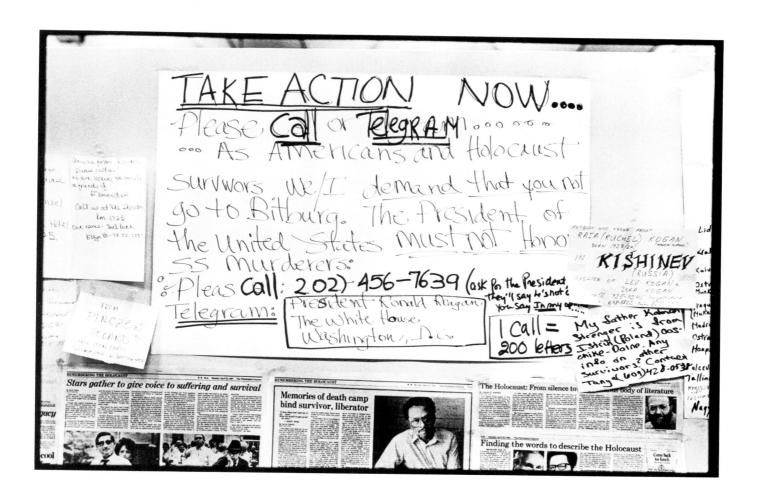

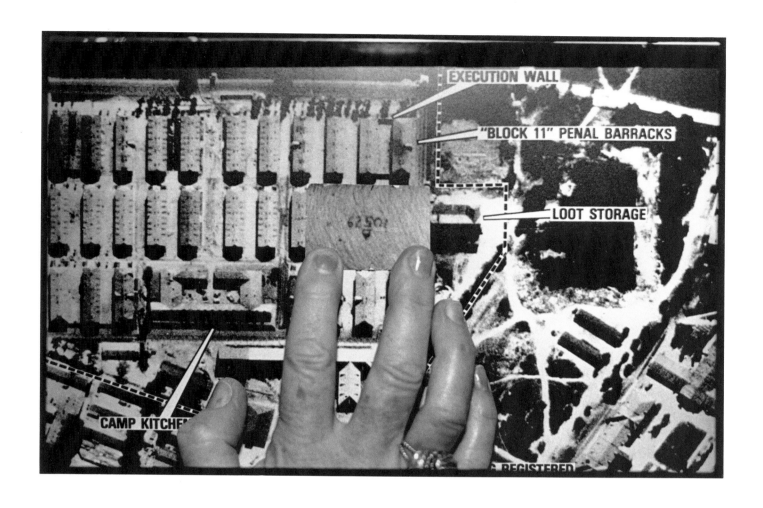

Illuminating the world of almost total darkness documented in Cohn's film, the citizens of the small, Nazi-occupied nation of Denmark stood tall in the autumn of 1943, refusing to give up their Jewish fellow citizens to the "final solution." For their noble conduct, which resulted in the survival of almost all of the estimated 8,000 Jews in Denmark at the time (about 75 percent of whom were Danish citizens), the people and government of Denmark were honored by the American Gathering and Federation in a ceremony on Monday morning. Ernest Michel, who first projected the idea of having a World Gathering of Jewish Holocaust Survivors (realized in Jerusalem in 1981), presided at the plenary session that morning. He is pictured here with Sam Bloch prior to introducing Roman Kent, who, as chairman of the board of directors, was to make the presentation of the "Shofar of Freedom" Award to the People and Government of Denmark.

"What they did was by their own accounts 'nothing extraordinary,'" said Roman Kent, addressing several thousand fellow survivors in Convention Hall. "But we know that the Holocaust was not an ordinary time. And in the world of the Holocaust, the ordinary was extraordinary, and that is why we are here to honor the Danish people." Everyone—the king and other royalty, government officials, clergymen, taxi drivers, school teachers, students, professors, shop owners, fishermen, doctors, lawyers, police, ordinary citizens of all ages from every walk of life—everyone, with few exceptions, participated in the rescue of their Jewish brothers and sisters during the crucial two or three weeks in October when the emergency occurred. This in a Christian country in which only one of about every 600 citizens was Jewish.

"The Danish people showed the world that the same instruments of government and diplomacy, that the same informal network of friends and neighbors that were used by the Nazis and their collaborators to kill people elsewhere," Roman continued, "could become an instrument of rescue and salvation in the hands of a people determined to remain moral. They showed what could have been done by others had they only cared." What they did, they did spontaneously, Roman continued. "When the Danes received the first word of Nazi plans for deportation, they sprang into action. Word was passed to each of the synagogues where Jews were assembled for Rosh Hashanah, the New Year services, and from building to building, from neighbor to neighbor, from friend to friend. Immediately, plans were formulated and effectively implemented to save all the Jews by evacuating them at once."

In his acceptance speech, Eigil Jørgensen, the Ambassador of Denmark, recalled how the rescue operation by boat was possible. "Denmark has the good fortune of having Sweden as its neighbor to the East," he said. "Only a narrow sound separates these two Scandinavian sister nations. Sweden had, much to our advantage, succeeded in maintaining her neutrality. Therefore, clandestine sea routes to Sweden had for some time been regularly operated by the Danish resistance. These were now expanded, and there was no difficulty in finding safe hiding places for our Jewish families until transport facilities were available. We knew the Swedes were prepared to receive the refugees and support them generously."

Earlier in his speech, the ambassador spoke of first reactions to the crisis. "There was not a second's doubt in the resistance movement and indeed in every quarter that a rescue operation was our paramount duty," he said. "A failure to act promptly would have been cowardice and meant immeasurable dishonor." The swift response produced near total success. "Only a few hundred who had for some reason not been warned, or in some cases refused to believe that the danger was imminent— and alas! one large group whose hiding place in a church loft was betrayed—fell into the hands of the Gestapo, and were deported, among them the chief rabbi,

Sam Bloch (l.), senior vice-president, American Gathering; Ernest Michel, honorary chairman, board of directors

Roman Kent (l.) presenting "Shofar of Freedom" Award to His Excellency Eigil Jørgensen, Ambassador of Denmark to the United States

who refused to escape until the whole community was safe." Even most of those deported were rescued toward the end of the war through the diplomatic efforts of the Swedish Count Folke Bernadotte and the Danish Red Cross. In remarkable contrast to what happened almost everywhere else, the Danish government officials joined neighbors of their absent Jewish countrymen in protecting their business properties, private dwellings, and personal belongings, so that, in Roman Kent's words, "when the Jews returned home, they had homes to return to."

The response of the Danes on behalf of their minority Jewish fellow-citizens stands as one of the greatest instances of human solidarity. According to the ambassador, however, the Danes themselves characterize their behavior rather differently: "We were grateful to be able to do our simple human duty."

Ambassador Jørgensen, interviewed in Convention Hall after accepting award

Elie Wiesel, recipient of the Nobel Peace Prize for 1986, before reading from "And the World Was Silent," Sunday evening

Waiting to testify, Civic Center

On the day before the presentation to the Danish people, I photographed Elie
Wiesel as he stood on stage in Convention Hall during the "Evening of Commemoration Through the Performing Arts," presented by the U.S. Holocaust Memorial
Council. He had just been introduced. I wondered what he might be thinking at
that moment, receiving the affirmation of several thousand fellow survivors exactly
forty years and eleven days after his own liberation from Buchenwald. He looked
a bit lost in the suit he was wearing, his head slightly bowed, his eyes—where?
"I wanted to see myself in the mirror," he wrote in *Night*, recalling an experience
several days after liberation. "I had not seen myself since the ghetto. From the
depths of the mirror, a corpse gazed back at me. The look in his eyes, as they
stared into mine, has never left me."

All survivors that night were looking into a mirror as they directed their gazes
and applause at Elie Wiesel. They saw not a corpse, but a living mirror held to the
world's face, a living symbol of their suffering and their hope, challenging us—no
matter what our past or present circumstances—to bear witness now with our
lives, to remember by creating a different, more just, world. Each one of us, together.

BUCHENWALD, JUNE 1945

Children who survived Buchenwald leave the camp for transport to rehabilitation in Switzerland enroute to Palestine.

The Survivors: To A New Life | 18

Buchenwald, 1945 (from "The Liberators," Center for Holocaust Studies [Brooklyn])

The photograph above shows children leaving Buchenwald in June 1945. The text reads: "Children who survived Buchenwald leave the camp for transport to rehabilitation in Switzerland en route to Palestine." Most of these child survivors look no older than you, Mark. Though some still wear striped caps and prison garb, you see nothing but joy in the faces of those boys as they head away from Buchenwald, not by cattle car to their planned deaths, but by passenger cars to freedom and new life. Elie Wiesel, sixteen at the time of liberation, was among the older boys sent out of the camp two months earlier. They were taken to an estate in Normandy, France, which had been converted to receive and house them for a while under the care of a Jewish Children's Aid Society, at the request of the French government. Within a year he was in Paris, beginning his studies and struggling to find a way to bear witness for both the living and the dead—the victims of the Holocaust. Only after ten years of observing a vow of silence did he find the voice that has ever since been that of a poet and prophet—challenging us to reach beyond our rigid frameworks to imagine, and begin building, a deeper, more universal peace. In his life, as in his stories, Elie Wiesel shows us the humanity and generosity of vision necessary to achieve such a goal.

Of the estimated half million Jewish refugees at the end of the War, about

Displaced Persons camps, 1945–46
(from "The Liberators," Center for Holocaust Studies [Brooklyn])

300,000 were survivors of the concentration camps. Most of them either were sent to, or found on their own, the DP camps set up to receive refugees in the American, British, and French occupation zones. Many of these DP camps were in the American zone in Germany and Austria.

The caption to the photo in the upper right corner, above, reads as follows: "At the Hillersleben Displaced Persons Camp, Chaplain Samuel Blinder takes the names and addresses of survivors seeking to be united with their American relatives." The photo in the lower right corner is captioned: "First Jewish babies born to survivors in the Fährenwald DP camp." And the photo on left: "Chaplain Eli Bohnen with child survivors in the Salzburg DP camp."

Most of the survivors I met at the Gathering had been in at least one of these "temporary" arrangements—in most cases for a year or two, often longer, and usually under very bleak conditions. Since Jews represented only about 25 percent of the total refugee population, they typically found themselves displaced among persons who had collaborated with the Nazis, actively or passively, or at least had remained indifferent to the Holocaust as it went on around them. Contributing to the ordeal of waiting was the fact that most of the world still did not want to take in Jews, survivors or not. The tragedy of the Jews thus continued; indeed, while

Max and Jackie Kahn at the Zachor Memorial, Civic Center

they were unwanted, many high-ranking Nazi war criminals and collaborators received favored treatment and a quick exit to safe havens outside of Germany during the immediate post-war years—notwithstanding the Nuremberg War Crimes Tribunal. Decades passed before this bitter irony was fully exposed and addressed. We continue to inherit the wounds of that political expediency even today, as seen in the cases of Klaus Barbie and other Nazi war criminals who have finally been brought to trial nearly half a century after their crimes.

Nothing brought home to me more poignantly the significance of Israel in the world of those displaced survivors of the Holocaust than the story of Max Kahn, though neither he nor his wife Jackie is a survivor. Max was twenty-four years old and working in his father's bakery in Shaker Heights, Cleveland, when Hitler invaded Poland. He enlisted in the army in 1941, trained as an air crew member in Witchita Falls, Texas, and eventually joined the 305th Bomb Group in Salt Lake City, Utah, early in 1942. The United States had by then entered the war, and by June Max found himself in Kettering, England, a U.S. military base about seventy-five miles northwest of London. He flew twenty-five B-17 bombing missions out of Kettering—seven over France, eighteen over Germany. Of these, six were night missions, the rest daylight; none had any fighter escorts over the target. "I'm thankful to be alive, to be honest with you," he said, explaining that the average life-span of such bombing crews was ten to fifteen missions.

What about the "Israel Air Force" T-shirt he was wearing? Back in Cleveland, after the war, Max had been approached by friends who asked if he wanted to go to Palestine to fight for the Jewish homeland created by the U.N.'s Partition Resolution, November 29, 1947. That year Max joined the air force unit of the Haganah, the original Jewish defense force before Israel declared its independence in May 1948. He flew combat missions over Damascas, Baghdad, Port Said, Rafa— about twenty missions in all. It was in Israel in August 1948, during the new state's defense against massive Arab invasion, that he first met survivors of the concentration camps. "I was on the airfield preparing for one of the last missions in the Negev desert, and I didn't have anybody to load the planes," Max recalled. "So I told this guy who was in charge of it, 'I need people here, otherwise I'm not going to be able to load the planes. . . .' So he said, 'I'll get you somebody.' The next morning I got up early and went out there, and I saw this . . . it was an army! There must have been 200 men! They had just brought them in from Cyprus. . . . Some of them were still undernourished, and they had bandages on their legs and arms. They hadn't recovered from their, you know, their wounds and things from the concentration camps. There must have been *at least* 200 of them, and they came marching onto the airfield. And those were the guys who helped me. They were survivors."

Three years after their liberation, these survivors were fighting in the War of Liberation of the State of Israel. Survivors of both the Nazi concentration camps in Europe and the British detention camps in Cyprus, they were fighting now against seven invading Arab armies. They were fighting so that they would never again be homeless, unwanted, or powerless: There would be Israel. "The way they were marching and singing after so long! They were so happy being in Israel and freedom—I will never forget it!" said Max Kahn, another kind of witness.

Although the vast majority of Jewish Holocaust survivors emigrated between 1945 and 1950 (an estimated 200,000 to Palestine and Israel alone), some stayed in Europe, but often not in the country of their birth. This was especially true of Polish Jews. Itka Zygmuntowicz, for example, was born and raised in Ciechanów, near Warsaw, but she lived in Sweden for eight years after the war before coming to the United States.

Itka Zygmuntowicz(r.), survivor of Auschwitz, with Barbro Jerring, Swedish Red Cross representative

Itka was sixteen years old when she arrived with her entire family at the gates of Auschwitz, where the words above the gate proclaimed: *Arbeit Macht Frei* (Work Makes One Free). "We were deceived in everything," she said. The Nazis had told them that they were being sent to a work camp, but the end was death, not freedom. "All your life you trust symbols! Facing the gate, on the right-hand side, was a truck with a red cross on it. I learned soon afterward that those who were led into the truck—among them my mother, younger brother, and little sister—went immediately to the gas chambers."

But Itka remained strong-willed and even more determined to live. "Whenever they called out my number, I would always say under my breath—'*Itka!* My name is *Itka!* You cannot take away my identity! . . .' Some people say, 'Why didn't you resist?' But resistance is relative to condition. Just *living* in such a hell was resisting. And not to become dehumanized—that was the greatest resistance!" Whether she lived or died during three years in Auschwitz, it was going to be with dignity, she told me. "Nobody can imprison your soul if you don't collaborate. And if you don't become evil yourself, nobody can ultimately destroy you."

After liberation, Itka remembers, some survivors at first refused to enter the

Barbro Jerring, witness from Stockholm

Swedish Red Cross trucks when they arrived in Malchow, a small town in northern Germany, to transport them out of the country. Only the attitude of their rescuers, their faces and manner, eased the survivors' residual fear of being deceived—like the kindly interest shown by this representative of the Swedish Red Cross, Barbro Jerring (personal secretary to Count Folke Bernadotte during the war), being thanked forty years later by a grateful survivor.

Family of Samuel Mitlas (father of Milton Mitlas)

"I have often wondered what might have happened to the photograph I posted at the Gathering," Milton Mitlas wrote to me in January 1987, several days after I had phoned him, wondering whether anyone had called him with the information that his notice had requested. "The photograph is of my father's family—his mother, brothers, sisters and their children—taken in the early 1930s. My father immigrated to this country about 1910 and settled in Omaha, Nebraska. . . . His six brothers and sisters who remained in Czestochowa, Poland, all perished in the Holocaust."

Mina Kalter (2nd from l.) with friends and fellow survivors

The only survivors were three of his father's nephews, all brothers, who came to America after the War. "They stayed in Philadelphia for a time, then moved West. I have since lost track of them and have not heard from them since my father's death."

Twenty-five years after his father died, Milton Mitlas, father of two grown children and proprietor of a bookstore, is still trying to locate those few relatives who can tell him what he wants to know about his family's experiences in Europe during the Holocaust. "I have had no response to the photograph till your call."

In July 1986, Mina Kalter returned to her hometown of Przeworsk in southeastern Poland for the first time since she escaped the ghetto there on her eighteenth birthday, March 15, 1941. She would have returned right after the war, but she and her husband, Sol (they had met in a Siberian labor camp), learned that some young

Jewish partisans who had survived and returned to her husband's hometown of Lezajsk, just north of her own hometown, had been killed when someone threw a bomb into their house. Warned by the only survivor of this tragedy, a severely crippled young man, and hearing of pogroms and other violence against returning Jews, they decided not to risk going back.

Mina estimates that there were about 7,500 Jews living in her hometown before the war. When she returned in 1986, there were none there, nor in her husband's town. "My home was no longer there—the area had been razed and totally rebuilt. Even in the cemetery, the tombstones had all been removed." She visited her mother's hometown of Grodzisko, hoping there to find some trace of her past. "One broken tombstone is all that remains," she said. "An eighty-six-year-old non-Jewish man named Jan Chmura lives on the outskirts of the town and gave us an account of the Jews. He had been in the burial unit for the Jews who were killed there—1,500 of them from some 500 families. The Nazis had rounded up all they could find, he told us, and then shot them right there in the cemetery. He took us around, pointing out every indentation in the ground—who was buried here, who there—he knew the names, including some of my own family. My husband said a prayer over the site."

It was only an eight-day trip, despite all they had to do. Their son and daughter were at their sides, having urged their parents to make the trip after Mina's recovery from open-heart surgery in 1984. They visited the Belzec and Auschwitz death camps, where they assume most of their families were murdered. Before returning to Warsaw for their flight back to the United States, they visited the only functioning synagogue in Cracow. Sol, a cantor, conducted a service on Shabbat for the eighteen Jews who continue to worship there. The youngest was about seventy years old; all were poor and alone. Why had these Jews remained in Poland? "In the beginning," Mina explained, "they stayed to hope for the return of family members; later, because they simply had no place to go."

Simon Rozenkier, who lost his parents, four sisters, and younger brother in the Holocaust, remains skeptical about ever returning to Poland and reliving his experiences, including many narrow escapes from death while surviving six camps. He was deported in 1940, at age twelve, from his hometown of Wloclawek, in central Poland, and liberated at Buchenwald by General George Patton's 3rd Armored Division on April 11, 1945. "So horrible were the thousands of corpses piled up, and the condition of the living," Simon recalled, "that General Eisenhower ordered the civilians from Weimar to come up and look. He was so mad at their claims of ignorance of what had been going on. They didn't want to look. And mothers put their hands over their children's eyes. 'Nein! Nein!' they kept saying."

In 1943 Simon was working in the Poznan labor camp at Kreisling, a large farm-estate converted into a manufacturing site for Fokke-Wolff fighter planes. Caught hiding a potato and a few carrots in the cuff of his pants one day, he was sentenced to be hanged the following week with two teenage friends, brothers from Lodz, who had been caught stealing bread. Others, too, including the father of the brothers, were charged with similar "crimes against the Third Reich" and scheduled to be hanged on the same day. "I was on the bench with twenty or so others," Simon remembers, "with the noose just placed around my neck, when the camp commander arrived on a motorcycle and ordered me released. 'You will die *working!*' the kapo [prisoner in charge of other prisoners] said as he took the rope off my neck." Later, Simon learned that his sister, who worked as a maid for the commander's wife in one of the adjacent camps, had heard of her brother's sentence and used her influence to intervene. She herself did not survive the war.

Simon told me about the insignia on his arm. He was a step-sergeant in the 79th Tank Battalion, Company "A," of the 25th ("Lightning") Infantry Division during the Korean War. He was wounded in an ambush near Pork Chop Hill in 1952.

Simon Rozenkier, survivor

Eva Bentley (l.), Dr. Laszlo Tauber, and Rose Jackson, survivors

"He saved my life!" Eva Bentley says of Dr. Laszlo Tauber, remembering the fall of 1944 in Budapest. This was the period of deepest crisis for the Jews of Hungary. While Adolf Eichmann personally supervised the Special Operation Unit for the liquidation of the Hungarian Jews, Raoul Wallenberg and others were trying desperately to save as many lives as possible.

On the night of October 16, 1944, Eva was brought to a makeshift Jewish hospital set up in a high school just outside the area of Jewish concentration. She was ten years old and suffering from a gunshot wound in the kidney. Like a hundred others that night, she had been a victim of the "Arrow Cross," a viciously pro-Nazi band of young Hungarian fascists. "There were not enough doctors or medicine in the hospital," she recalled. "Laszlo operated all day and all night until he fell off his feet. He lived on nothing but hot water and tea and slept on the floor, insisting that every available bedding be used for the sick and injured." His compassion gave them strength as he worked heroically to save as many lives as possible. "I remember once turning my head weakly," Eva said, "and seeing him crying, holding the hand of a dying patient."

She didn't see him again until twenty-five years later at a reunion in New York City on the fiftieth anniversary of the school in Budapest that each had once attended. At the Gathering she introduced Laszlo to her childhood friend, Rose Jackson of Sighet. Rose's father, Ludwig Silber, had owned a jewelry store in Sighet, the small town where Eva would visit her grandparents for three months every

Mother and daughter, survivors of Nowy Sacz, Poland

summer. "I was twelve years old, Eva four, when we first met in 1938." Deceptively, the Holocaust passed over both Sighet and Budapest during the early war years, and Eva's summer vacations continued uninterrupted. The rude awakening to disaster did not occur until the spring of 1944. Rose, eighteen years old and newly wed at the time, recalled the shock: "We were married in Sighet in February, honeymooned in Budapest in March, and arrived home—to be deported to Auschwitz in April."

Alex Steinberg, survivor of Mauthausen

For seventy-year-old Alex Steinberg, a survivor of Mauthausen, and his wife, Esther, a survivor of Auschwitz, Stutthof, and Ravensbrück concentration camps, it was the Bitburg controversy that finally sparked their "coming out" as survivors. Journeying to Philadelphia for the Gathering was their first public statement. "We wanted to meet people and to express our anger that Reagan was going to Bitburg," they told me two years later. Their voices still trembled with outrage. For

Wolf Pasmanik, founder, American Holocaust Committee to Erect a Monument in New York in Honor of the Six Million Jewish Martyrs

them, the president's trip was a symbol of amnesia, not of reconciliation. The implications of his action remain clear—and disturbing. "I feel bitter," Alex said of the hundreds of books, pamphlets, and other writings that declare the Holocaust an exaggeration or fabrication. "If they're denying it now—right in our faces, denying it!—what about a hundred years from now?"

Irina, daughter, and . . .

Remember, Mark, how charmed we were by Irina's daughter, Karina, when she sang those little songs in Russian and danced her ballet steps at your eleventh birthday party a few months after the Gathering? Karina was born on February 16, 1980, a few hours after her mother arrived in Philadelphia from Kiev, one of several thousand Jews allowed to emigrate from the Soviet Union that year. Although Karina's grandparents, Izya and Rosa Rabinovich, couldn't speak a word of English, they followed two years later, to be near their only child and grandchild.

. . . Karina, granddaughter of survivors, at Civic Center fountain

In July 1941, Izya was a twenty-year-old soldier preparing for the defense of Leningrad against the Germans. Two months later the Germans would lay siege to the city, eventually cutting off all rail lines and virtually every other supply route. By the end of the year, as many as two or three thousand citizens per day were dying of starvation. Rosa, meanwhile, left the university in Kiev and joined the thousands of others who were fleeing or being evacuated as the German invasion swept toward the city. Rosa's four grandparents stayed behind with other relatives.

Adina Fried Stern (l.) and Sara Fried Engelman, sisters from Sighet

In all, about 100,000 Jews remained in Kiev, mainly women, children, the old, and the sick. Able-bodied Jewish men, like Izya, were in the Red Army.

Two months later, while Izya was battling the Germans in the famous 900-Day Siege of Leningrad and Rosa was toiling in a labor camp in Siberia, many of their relatives and friends were among the estimated 37,000 Jews of Kiev massacred in a thirty-six-hour period, September 29–30, at Babi Yar, a huge ravine just outside the city. Sitting in the living room of their small apartment in Philadelphia, the family album opened to photographs of Irina and Karina, Rosa rocked slowly in her seat, holding her head and moaning at the memories being stirred: "If I not go to Siberia, I will be in Babi Yar!"

Adina Fried was so near death when British soldiers pulled her emaciated body out from among the corpses at Bergen-Belsen in May 1945, that a full week passed in the hospital before she was even aware she had been liberated. Meanwhile, her sister Sara, who had frantically directed the soldiers to the barrack where Adina lay dying, had herself become deathly ill and was hospitalized elsewhere a few days later. Inseparable in the ghetto in Sighet, in the Auschwitz death camp, and at Bergen-Belsen, they were separated now for the first time.

Several weeks later they were reunited by a British doctor who found Adina among the thousands of hospitalized survivors and had her transferred to the hospital where Sara was recovering from typhus. Soon afterward the sisters were

Helen and Adam Schwartz, survivors from Lodz and Tuczyn, Poland

in Sweden and recuperating. "I always thank the Swedish government for saving us," Sara says, even today. "If we hadn't been able to go there, how would they have ever coped with so many sick in Germany?"

Of Elie Wiesel, their brother Arie's childhood friend in Sighet, Adina says: "God gave him the strength to relate our story." In 1975, Sara returned to their hometown of Sighet to visit the grave of their mother, who died before the war. Their father, like the hundreds of thousands of others who died in Auschwitz, has no grave. That day, Sara also saw her former school, and the house where they had once lived. Ultimately, like Elie Wiesel after a similar journey in 1964, Sara determined that she would never return again: "Too much has changed. There is nothing there for us."

Photojournalists Carol Bernson and Stephen Shames making portraits of survivors at the Civic Center

Two friends posing for snapshots, the Civic Center fountain

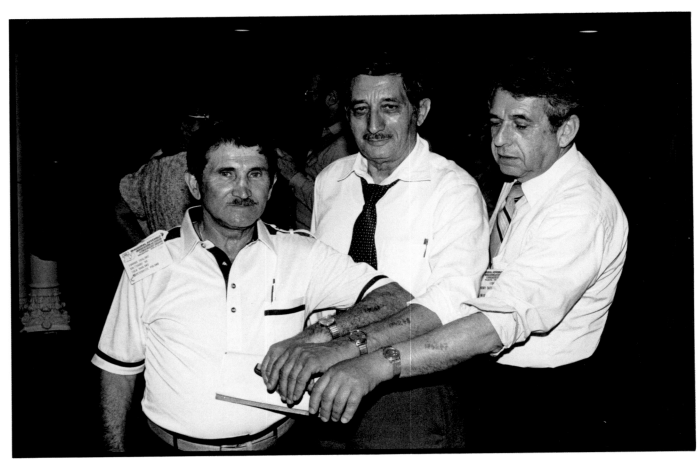

Three survivors of Auschwitz

The three survivors pictured in the photograph above met accidentally in Philadelphia after nearly forty years. Ed Smolarz (left) spoke to me about it. "I recognized him (William Schiff, center) at the Monument—'Hey, William!' I shouted—he didn't recognize me at first." They hadn't seen each other since 1948. "We used to play soccer together in the same DP camp after the war, and we were on the same boxing team." The third survivor was not recognized until someone in a group gathered in Survivors' Village remarked how rare it was to see consecutive numbers. "I hadn't got to know him so well," Ed recalled, "but we were all from Cracow in the first transport to Auschwitz." The numbers read: 174247, 174248, 174250. The missing number belonged to Ed's best friend, Dolek Waldman, who was shot while attempting to escape with Ed and four others on a death march from Auschwitz early in 1945.

Images of book-burnings during *Kristallnacht* flashed through my mind when I first saw two men in Survivors' Village examining a couple of Yiddish books at a small cart. The widespread destruction of such literature during the twelve years of the Third Reich was another aspect of the Nazi attempt to extinguish every form of Jewish life. It gave special pleasure to many survivors at the Gathering to see these books for sale from the National Yiddish Book Center in Amherst, Massachusetts. The non-profit center was founded in 1980 for the purpose of preserving, restoring, and making available to people worldwide over half a million volumes

"The Book Peddler"

of new, used, rare, and out-of-print works in Yiddish, periodically described in their newsletter, *Der Pakn-Treger* ("The Book Peddler").

Bess Katz of the Sholom Aleichem Club of Philadelphia explained why she and other club members volunteered to organize the Yiddish Book Center's presence at the Gathering: "We wanted to give survivors encouragement that not all is lost of their Eastern European culture, that there is some kind of continuity. Survivors need not look back only to what was lost. To look ahead has become possible. There is a renewed future for Yiddish."

Kathryn and Steve Berkowitz (above), and Manya and Barry Piels, second generation

Rose and Aron Goldstein, survivors

Kathryn Berkowitz was six months pregnant when this photograph (l., top) was made at the Civic Center. Her husband Steve, son of survivors Jack and Gail Berkowitz, wanted their third-generation child to be there so that they could tell him (Jonathan, born July 26, 1985) when he grows up that he, too, had actually attended this important fortieth anniversary event.

Manya Piels—named after her grandmother, Manya Offenberger, who died in the Holocaust—is the second-generation person in the bottom photograph. She and her husband Barry live in Fairfield, Connecticut. Manya's father, Israel Korngold, who survived Belzec after being deported there from a small town near Lublin, died the month before the Gathering at age eighty-five. Manya came to Philadelphia out of a special commitment to his memory.

Aron Goldstein, a retired tailor, and his wife Rose first met in a DP camp in Austria in 1945 and were married that same year. He survived Auschwitz after the liquidation of the Lodz Ghetto in 1944. Rose, a Czech Jew, survived three camps, including Auschwitz. Both lost their parents and many other relatives in the Holocaust and felt a deep moral obligation to be at the Gathering. "As long as one of us is still alive," Aron explained, "no one can say it didn't happen."

"We were used for germ warfare studies," stated Eva Kor of Terre Haute, Indiana, on Monday morning at the Civic Center. She and eight other twins had come to testify against Josef Mengele before a special Senate subcommittee at the Gathering. Eva is founder and executive director of CANDLES, an acronym for "Children of Auschwitz-Nazis' Deadly Lab Experiments Survivors," an international group of "Mengele Twins" formed in 1983 and numbering over 130 members in twelve countries. Mengele is the notorious SS officer and chief physician of Auschwitz who performed bizarre genetic and other experiments on the camp's helpless inmates. His most cherished victims were twins, most of whom were children. Eva Kor, a Hungarian Jew, was only nine years old at the time. "We were injected with germs and exotic diseases," Eva recalled. "We were used as Mengele's guinea pigs." After injecting the twins (only one of each pair) with these deadly microbes, Mengele and his staff would study their fever charts. "They would kill the other twin with a chloroform shot to the heart as soon as one twin died, then do autopsies, comparing diseased and nondiseased organs." Mengele, whom inmates called "the Angel of Death," also made crude attempts to change the brown eye-color of certain children who had otherwise blond, "Aryan" features. He injected their eyes with a blue dye but succeeded only in producing extraordinary pain in his victims and devastating psychological effects. Blindness resulted in some cases, and even death, according to Robert Jay Lifton in his book, *The Nazi Doctors* (1986).

Irene Hizme spent two and a half years in Theresienstadt (Terezin), a concentration camp in Czechoslovakia, before she and her twin brother were sent to Auschwitz in 1943 at the age of five and a half. Both survived some of Mengele's experiments. Elias Malek was the youngest of the four twins pictured here when he was subjected to Mengele's "research." He was three years old.

Peter Somogyi was eleven years old when he was deported from Pecs, a town in southern Hungary near the Yugoslavian border. He arrived at Auschwitz in July 1944 with his mother, sister, and twin brother, Tom. "We were in line for the gas chamber," he recalled, "though of course none of us knew it at the time." He remembers a Nazi officer walking alongside the lines asking, *'Zwillinge? Zwillinge?"* (Twins? Twins?) "No one came forward," Peter told me, "and my mother said nothing until the third time he came around." His brother and he then walked off with Dr. Mengele.

I was surprised at first to hear that his mother had spoken out. Was it possible she had intuited the destination of the line they were in? Or had she felt that by dividing the four of them she increased the odds that someone would survive? "I've wondered, too, but I'll never know," said Peter. "All I know is that if she had said nothing, I would have ended up in the gas chamber." And why had she waited for the third passing of the "Angel of Death"? Wondering if Mengele's *manner* had affected her final decision, I asked Peter if he could recall Mengele's tone of voice as he asked for *Zwillinge.* Had it been harsh and demanding? I asked, mimicking the tone. Or gentle . . . "Yes, like that!" said Peter. "He asked *nicely, very nicely.* Mengele was always very polite, you know. . . ."

"He couldn't convince the rest of his family to believe the rumors," Peggy Goldman said of her father, Sam Margolis, a Polish Jew from the little town of Kremenets. "So he and a friend fled. An older brother, Efraim, had left before him and had joined the Russian army in order to fight the Nazis. He was an absolutely fearless man who won many medals for bravery."

The only other family member who escaped was her Uncle Zalman—one of those who had stayed behind. He hid in a field owned by farmers who were Jehovah's Witnesses, one of the groups targeted for murder by the Nazis. (Gypsies, homosexuals, Russian prisoners of war, Polish intelligentsia, Spanish republicans,

''Mengele Twins'' (Elias, Peter, Eva, Irene)

Peggy Goldman, daughter of survivors

and the mentally and physically disabled were others.) When the Jehovah's Witnesses discovered him, they took him into their home. "Then they hid him in a hole in the ground in the backyard of their farmhouse," Peggy said. "They fixed it up to make it look like a grave. They fed him, and he stayed hidden like this for a year. It was the Christian thing to do, they believed."

Peggy's parents first met near the Soviet-Iranian border, where each had fled to escape the Nazi invaders in 1941. They married in 1944 and, after liberation in January 1945, returned to Poland in search of relatives. Peggy was born in June of that year in Lodz. That same month they escaped from the Russians, who were closing Poland behind what later came to be called the "Iron Curtain" (Winston Churchill's phrase) of Communist-occupied Europe. With hundreds of other survivors, they made their way by train and on foot to Austria, posing as Greek refugees.

Brigitta and Barth Aaron and children, second-generation family

Peggy's mother, Rae Margolis, recalled the ordeal's end: "I was carrying her with my breast in her mouth almost all of the time. We were exhausted, all of us, and starving when we finally arrived in Salzburg. The first American I ever saw in my life was a tall Black man, a soldier. Seeing a baby in rags, he took Peggy in his arms and kissed her. There were tears running down his face. Maybe he had children of his own at home."

Rosa Lantinberg, survivor, and her husband, Louis

Rosa Lantinberg was born in Warsaw but lived in Lublin most of her life before being deported in 1941 to the nearby death camp at Majdanek. She escaped the same year and was kept safe from the Nazis by Christian friends in Lublin, Warsaw, and several other places. "Many, many very good friends saved me," she said to me in a soft voice over the phone from her home in Tucson, Arizona. She is seventy-seven years old now. Rosa and her husband Louis have one child, a daughter, who is President of the Second Generation, Sons and Daughters of Holocaust Survivors, on Staten Island, New York. Of the seventy-eight members of her extended family at the time of the Holocaust, Rosa is the only one who survived.

"The past lives within us, whether we admit it or not," Isabella Katz Leitner said, "but my past is so *insane* that it looms larger than any other past because it has these images of totally abnormal daily happenings—like the stench of 15,000 people being burned each day at Auschwitz. And I live with that scent in my nostrils." Isabella and two of her sisters survived by escaping while on a death march to Bergen-Belsen in January 1945, after their evacuation from Auschwitz. They are from the small town of Kisvarda in northeastern Hungary. On May 31, 1944, when they and the rest of their family arrived at Auschwitz, their mother and

Isabella Katz Leitner, survivor of Auschwitz

little sister were immediately directed to their deaths by a mere flick of Mengele's wrist. He had been conducting the "selection" on that day when the transport from Kisvarda pulled into Birkenau—the major killing site at Auschwitz—and began unloading boxcars of Jews for immediate division into two lines. One line constituted a death sentence for those in it: mothers with young children, elderly people, the sick and lame—all destined for the gas chambers or fire pits. The other line meant "life"—in reality only the "opportunity" to be worked to death, becoming the *Muselmänner* ("walking skeletons") of future selections. Unless somehow one survived—as did Rachel, Chicha, and Isabella Katz.

"You have your memories of childhood," Isabella said, "and I have those too, the normal memories of childhood harmony and dissonance, school life, and decisions to make—I have all of that, like you. But then there is another entire layer that's called 'Auschwitz,' right underneath the skin. You can't get rid of it. It will never go away." For thirty years she wrote scattered pieces of a diary, quarrying the deep layer of pain that never goes away. She threw away many fragments at first, but soon began accumulating others, in a shoebox. These became the material for a small but powerful book of memoirs, *Fragments of Isabella*, published in 1978 and followed in 1985 by another volume, *Saving the Fragments*.

In her New York apartment over a year after the Gathering, that layer of pain called "Auschwitz" was especially palpable. "I was talking to my sister Rachel today," Isabella told me, "and she said, 'I don't sleep, maybe four hours, five maximum. You know where I learned not to sleep? In Auschwitz. I never went to sleep because I was afraid I'm going to wake up dead. So I was afraid to go to sleep!' It's true. She's totally an insomniac. She was afraid they'll haul her off to the crematorium in her sleep. She had to stay watch, to be alert enough so that if Mengele came in the middle of the night she could run for her life. It broke my heart. I didn't know. . . . Every once in a while somebody in the family will drop such a sentence that will bring back a whole world of misery. For those who say, 'Forget it! It happened long ago!'—Well, it *didn't* happen long ago. It's *today,* standing in the kitchen this morning talking to my poor little sister. 'Poor little sister' who's pushing sixty now! Forty-two years later she can't sleep because she learned how not to sleep in Auschwitz!"

The people in the photograph (r., top) are examining the Arnold Shay Collection of Holocaust Artifacts, one of the exhibits at the Civic Center during the weekend. Arnold Shay of Bedzin is a member of the Association of Jewish Holocaust Survivors in Philadelphia. He recently published a book about his experiences during the Holocaust, entitled *Hell Was My Home*. He startled me one day near the time of the first photo exhibition of my work by stating that not everyone went to Auschwitz by cattle car: "I went there by limousine," he said, his eyes reflecting the irony of this surprising detail.

Arnold had been active with resistance forces from the very beginning of the Nazi occupation of Poland, and by 1943 had already escaped from the Gestapo several times when he was finally caught along with two other ghetto fighters. The Gestapo officers were unwilling to risk sending them to Auschwitz by cattle car with thousands of other Jews, fearing they might escape yet again, so Arnold and his companions were driven to the death camp in a black SS limo. Once imprisoned behind the gates of Auschwitz, he was required to wear the letters "I. L." on his striped shirt. The letters stand for *Im Lager* ("inside the prison"), which meant that the prisoner was not allowed outside the camp in slave labor units.

Arnold's collection of Holocaust artifacts ranges from original artwork by inmates to gruesome evidence of their fate—such as an urn of ashes from the crematoria and the long, dark braids cut from the head of a young Jewish girl.

Survivors and students viewing the Arnold Shay Collection of Holocaust Artifacts, Civic Center

Documentary footage of the death camps, closed-circuit TV, Civic Center

"'Ruchale!' I yelled," said Susan Niederman. "She recognized me and called out, 'Rifchu!'—the nickname for Rachel, my middle name. We came from Germany as orphans. There were about thirty of us on the ship. We hadn't seen each other for thirty-eight years." Susan and Ruchale spent several months together in a children's home in New York after arriving in America in 1947, both of them teenagers. Their chance reunion in Survivors' Village could not have occurred before 1983, Susan told me, for it was only in that year that she decided to share her experiences as a survivor and to seek out others. "Until the Washington Gathering in 1983, I barely spoke about it, even to my children. I swallowed all that pain, and buried it." I asked her what changed her mind. "The mere fact of realizing that we're not going to be around forever. I must do it now, I told myself, while there's still time—no matter what the pain." Unburdening herself has helped others, too. "Now I help give new beginnings to people who have lost hope, people who think that they have nothing to live for," Susan says of her work with blind and partially sighted adults in New York. "I have that ability to help create new interests and hope in people, because I too knew the greatest darkness—and began again."

Susan was fifteen years old in 1944 when she reached the gates of Auschwitz with her parents, sister, and three brothers. Only she and her oldest brother, Mayer, survived the camp, but they were never reunited. "I looked for him all over Europe right after the war, until a friend of his recognized me and told me that he had been with my brother to the very end. Mayer had been so starved that even though he was liberated, he couldn't carry on. My brother lasted as long as he did because he had heard that I was alive. He had hopes of seeing me."

How did Susan manage to survive? "My naïveté and unsophisticated knowledge of the world led me to be more hopeful than those older than me who knew better," she said. "I accepted what happened. I thought: Well, when you're fifteen, I guess this is the way you live, and then things get better. Also, I was so skinny as a kid that I had very little to lose when I got to Auschwitz. I wasn't big enough to make the labor force, so they put me to work instead opening suitcases and sorting out shirts, shoes, jewelry, and so forth. We did this in Birkenau, about 200 feet from one of the crematoria."

She smelled the burning flesh from the smokestack above the building that swallowed long lines of people every day and saw that only their clothes emerged. Had her mother been in one of those lines when they were separated? "After I understood what was happening, every woman's face looked like my mother's— I was so desperate to find her alive!" Susan remembers. "I was going from one person to the next, asking, 'Are you my mommy?' and 'Do you know where my mommy is?' One woman said to me, 'You see that chimney over there? That's where your mother is!' But another took me aside. 'No, my child,' she answered. 'I'm not your mommy, but you must be strong. . . .'"

The closest her strength came to giving out was on a death march from Auschwitz. "The Russians were very close. We were evacuated and forced to march for days and days. I was freezing, wearing only a stupid dress and a pair of old shoes." At one point she drifted wearily back toward the end of the long column of marchers, unable to keep up the pace. Those who collapsed or couldn't keep up were shot on the spot, leaving a grim trail of death. Many who had survived the death camp itself broke down finally on this march away from it. "'I might as well give up,' I thought for the very first time. I was freezing, starving, completely demoralized—beyond hope finally. Suddenly this wagon drawn by two horses came from behind—probably a local farmer as much surprised as we were. On instinct alone, I and a few others ran after the wagon, hoping to get on. I was holding on with one hand when I suddenly felt myself being picked up and thrown into the wagon by a person behind me who then also got on. The wagon rode all the way toward the front of the line with three or four of us huddled together in a corner under a blanket of some kind. When it got near the front—about two

Chance reunion, Survivors' Village: Susan (r.), and Ruchale

kilometers down the line—I was pushed off by the others as they jumped. The driver would not have been allowed to pass the beginning of the line without his wagon being checked. So there I was, near the front again, which gave me renewed hope—though not much more energy. By the time I had fallen back again, trains were waiting for us and took us to Bergen-Belsen."

"Maybe someone can tell me where their graves are," reads the sign around the neck of Sam Shatz, who is at the microphone. I had seen him in tears on the day of the Memorial Service, and once or twice afterward, but I didn't get to talk with him until I saw him in Survivors' Village, singing Yiddish folk songs in a spirited session with fellow survivors and friends. We have talked several times since.

Sam is a native of Bilgoraj, a small town about fifty miles south of Lublin in

Sam Shatz (l.), survivor from Bilgoraj, Poland

southeastern Poland. He and his mother, little sister, and two brothers fled Bilgoraj separately in 1939, only days before the Germans occupied the town. They were reunited inside Russia and moved to Kirovograd near the southern port city of Odessa, where they lived undisturbed for the next two years. Sam, then fifteen years old, attended school every day and made new friends. On June 22, 1941, however, Germany attacked the Soviet Union, and within weeks the Germans were only a few miles outside Kirovograd. "City officials gave orders that all people not old enough to fight should evacuate," Sam told me. "Passenger trains had been used for troop transport, so the only trains left to evacuate citizens were cattle cars. We left everything behind and got on the last train out."

One of his brothers remained behind, recovering in the hospital from a wound received during one of the German bombing raids. Several hours into their eastward journey, the train stopped at a small station and Sam's other brother got down from the car momentarily to get some water for their ailing and exhausted mother. He had not yet returned when the train started pulling out—too quickly for him to catch up. "My mother was screaming, pulling her hair out in despair," Sam remembers. He himself was separated from his mother and sister a few days after their train arrived in the region of Rostov, about seventy-five miles northeast of Moscow. Hoping to relieve his mother's grief over the loss of her other son, Sam tried to get to Rostov, naïvely hoping that train officials there might help him locate

Survivors singing Yiddish folksongs in Survivors' Village

his missing brother. The way was blocked halfway into his journey, however, because of heavy troop and supply movement in the area causing trains to be cancelled, re-routed, or requisitioned by Red Army Command for use in the defense of Moscow. In a moment of panic, he boarded any train he could—only to find himself arrested for having insufficient identification papers. Many trains and cities later, he ended up in Siberia, where he was put to work in the coal mines of Stalinsk until the end of the war.

After the war he returned to Poland but found Warsaw and Cracow in ruins. He then learned that one of only four relatives left after the war had been murdered in the Kielce pogrom in July 1946, so he decided to stay near Warsaw instead of returning to Bilgoraj. He joined with other survivors to form a kibbutz, which they maintained until the summer of 1947, when they fled Poland through Czechoslovakia, toward Italy, on a perilous journey to Palestine.

"There were 450 of us on a boat built for much less than half that many," Sam said. "We were put in like sardines—hot, sweating, nauseous. It was a terrible two-week trip from Italy to Palestine, completely illegal, and finally we were caught through a spy in our own boat—a young British girl who spoke Yiddish and Hebrew. . . . We were surrounded by a British fleet. They yelled over loudspeakers: 'Give up! We will not hurt you!' Two guys got killed in a fight before they brought all of us to Haifa, then to the concentration camp in Cyprus."

Sam joined the Israeli Navy as soon as he finally reached the country in 1949. Five years later he came to the United States. "When I left Bilgoraj there were two hundred people in my family. My mother's brother had twelve children. A big, big family we were. It is forty-five years since I lost them," he said, "but in my heart I feel, as long as I am alive, I'm still with hope that somebody will be able to tell me something about my loved ones."

Even if only where they're buried? I asked. "In Israel in 1981, and in Washington, my hope was to find someone alive. But in Philadelphia I no longer expected that. I hoped only to find someone who maybe knew where their graves are."

David Fishel was a boy of thirteen living in Bedzin when four Gestapo officers came to take him away together with other children in a round-up early in 1942. They found him hiding under his bed in the one room that he, his mother, and his two sisters had been forced to share. After a struggle that ended with a rifle-butt to his mother's stomach, David was dragged screaming from the apartment building—never to see his mother or sisters again. He survived two labor camps before being sent to Blechhammer, a subsidiary camp of Auschwitz, where he remained until December 1944. After evacuations and death marches from Auschwitz, Gross Rosen, and Buchenwald, he hid himself for three days among the unburied corpses at Langerstein, a sub-camp of Buchenwald—unwilling and virtually unable to take another step, so emaciated and exhausted had he become. He was liberated on the fourth day by American troops.

Now fifty-seven years old, David owns and operates "Fishel's Skywalk Deli" in Des Moines, Iowa, where he and his wife, Louise, have lived since their marriage thirty-six years ago. They have two children and three grandchildren. But even after forty-five years, David says that he sometimes wakes up screaming in the middle of the night, reliving the day they dragged him away from his mother.

I met Nora Levin in Survivors' Village with her friend, Mary Costanza, and two survivors with whom they were talking. Mary wrote an important book, *The Living Witness: Art in the Concentration Camps and Ghettos* (1982), and she herself, a Gentile, has made many paintings and drawings using Holocaust history and themes. Some of her work is exhibited at Yad Vashem, and some was on display at the Gathering, along with paintings, sculpture, and works in other media by survivors and children of survivors in an exhibition organized by Jean Bloch Rosensaft.

Nora is Professor of Jewish History at Gratz College and Director of the Gratz Holocaust Oral History Archive, which she founded in 1979. At the Gathering, Nora, together with Ellen Rofman and Josey Fisher, coordinated the interviewing of 300 survivors who were willing to tell what happened to them and their families during the Holocaust. Their tapes are now part of the Gratz Archive and available for use by scholars, researchers, students, and others who wish to understand more about

David Fishel, survivor

Nora Levin (2nd from r.) and Mary Costanza (2nd from l.) with survivors

this darkest period in human history. Nora is a totally committed teacher and scholar who is devoted to understanding among peoples, especially in regard to the causes, history, and implications of the Holocaust. Since 1968, when her first book, *The Holocaust: The Destruction of European Jewry, 1933–1945,* was published, she has written other works and lectured on the Holocaust, Soviet Jewry, and Christian-Jewish relations. She is on the board of the Inter-Faith Council on the Holocaust. Twelve years ago, Nora helped the Philadelphia School District to develop curricula on the Holocaust—the first in the country and a model ever since for school districts throughout the nation.

Renee Duering and her daughter, Naomi, had never really talked much about Renee's experiences in the camps; by the time the Gathering ended, this had changed. At the Holocaust exhibition at the National Museum of American Jewish History, Renee, a German Jew from Cologne, pointed out the barrack where she had lived in Auschwitz after deportation from Holland—she had fled there before that country, too, came under Nazi control in May–June 1940. Renee then placed a small photograph of her prisoner number over the location on the display photo. She had had the number removed from her arm years ago because she didn't like the stares and questions it so often evoked. I suggested making a photograph of Renee and Naomi together, Renee holding the number against her arm where it

Naomi (r.) and her mother, Renee, survivor of Auschwitz

had once been. They liked this idea, but Naomi suddenly suggested (with no objection from her mother or me) that *she* hold the number in place, and so she did—clasping her mother's arm as you see in the photograph. Not long after they had returned to their homes in the San Francisco area, Naomi wrote to me, telling how the Gathering had affected her: "Now more than ever the meaning of my life has changed. My mother is very special to me and I hope to begin [a] book soon. I plan to write down her story. . . ."

Young girl, Survivors' Village

Joseph Schwarzbaum, survivor

Lucille and Sol Goldstein at the Zachor Memorial

Lucille had a stroke two years before the Gathering, and Sol had just recovered from open-heart surgery and was still in pain, but it would have taken more than that to have kept them from attending the ceremonies and events in Philadelphia—"and we'll be at the next Gathering in Miami," Lucille stated firmly. "We think it's important," she added, in a tone of quiet conviction. "We think the work is terribly important." Sol is the survivor, not Lucille, though their commitment is identical. Sol

Three generations

spent several years in Auschwitz, deported there at the age of thirteen from the town of Ciechanów. He lost his mother, father, and two brothers in the Holocaust.

Martin and Tibor survived the concentration camp outside Sered, Slovakia (a separate state created out of eastern Czechoslovakia in March 1939 by Hitler). Tibor escaped and joined partisans in the area until liberation by the Russians in February

Martin Zapletal (l.) and Tibor Capla, survivors from Slovakia

1945. Martin, whose Jewish mother, Yohanna Weiss of Nitra, had died before the War, survived by virtue of his being what the Nazis termed a *Mischling*—a person of so-called "mixed Jewish blood." Martin's father, a Slovakian Christian, got his only child released from the camp immediately upon returning from Hamburg at the end of 1944. According to Martin, his father had been working in Hamburg for the German war effort along with many other Slovakians sent abroad for that purpose under a political agreement earlier in the war. Martin's wife, Margita, had been deported to Auschwitz at the time of their separation in October 1944—two months pregnant. She was among the inmates driven out of the camp in a death march that began on January 17. Two weeks later, near Legnica in southwestern Poland, the Russians liberated the survivors. Margita was immediately hospitalized in the nearby city, and on May 14, 1945, five days after the end of the war in Europe had been declared, she gave birth to a son, Peter. Tibor's wife, Frantyska, also survived Auschwitz, after being subjected to the sterilization experiments of Dr. Carl Clauberg in "Block 10." Only after many miscarriages, and at great risk, was she able to bear their only child, Tomos, in 1950. Tibor and Frantyska now have two grandchildren.

Martin and his family lived in Czechoslovakia until 1966, when they immigrated to the United States. A few years ago, he and his wife completed a seven-year project of assembling documents and photographs for a 44-page oversize "Album of the Tragedy of the Jews of Slovakia." The estimated 75,000 Jews murdered by

Eli Okon (l.) and Harry Seder, survivors from Bialystok

the Nazis and their collaborators represents 85 percent of the population of Jews in Slovakia at the beginning of 1940.

"We play gin rummy—10 cents a game," Harry Seder, seventy-eight, told me. "We see a show once in a while and go to meetings. We have a very good friendship." Like his friend, Eli Okon, Harry was born in Bialystok, northeastern Poland, a city of about 100,000 people (60 percent Jews) when it was occupied by Red Army forces at the end of September 1939. (In a secret, pre-war arrangement, Stalin and Hitler had agreed to divide Poland between them after it had fallen to the Nazis.)

Harry and Eli lived in the same neighborhood in Bialystok. Eli, twelve years younger, used to go to school with Harry's nephew. That nephew survived, and two brothers, but no one else from Harry's extended family of more than one hundred people. Eli is the grandfather of Meredith Okon, one of the three children in the Monument photograph earlier. He worked in his father's bakery in Bialystok before the ghetto and deportations to Treblinka, where both his parents perished. Except for one sister who had emigrated to the United States in 1928, Eli, youngest of the seven brothers and sisters, alone survived the Holocaust. He and his wife, Marta, met in Kaufering, a sub-camp of Dachau. Near the end of the war, all 800 inmates were driven on a forced march toward Bavaria and the Tyrol. When the few who were left after ten days were met by American troops near Wolfratshausen,

Bavaria, they discovered that they were finally free. Marta remembered: "It was the most beautiful sight I have ever seen in my life! An American tank with soldiers tossing us chocolate, chewing gum—whatever they had!"

After eleven years working as an ambulance driver in Israel, Eli brought his family to the United States in 1960 and returned to the bakery profession that his father had taught him back in the 1930s. He retired two years ago in order to devote more time to his family (which now includes five grandchildren) and to his friend Harry.

Though only fourteen years old, "I was strong and looked sixteen," said Friedka Goodrich, remembering her arrival at Auschwitz in August 1944, in one of the last deportations from the Lodz Ghetto. After only three days in the camp, she was chosen together with 300 other women for transport to a concentration camp in the mountainous outskirts of Nohod, Czechoslovakia. Each day they crossed the German border into Bad-Kudowa, where they worked twelve hours in a factory that manufactured engine parts for German fighter planes. Eight months later they were liberated by the Russians. Friedka eventually learned that she was the sole survivor of a family that included her grandmother, both parents, four brothers and a sister, and many aunts, uncles, and cousins.

Friedka's husband, Stanley, is also the only one of his entire family to survive. At fifteen, he was the oldest of three children of an Orthodox Jewish family living in Nowy Targ, a small town in the Carpathian Mountains of southernmost Poland. "I lost my father on the first day of the war. It was five or six in the morning. Hundreds of men just started running away at news of the invasion. My father left with them to go east." Fifty-three German army divisions had attacked along the western border, and Cracow, just fifty miles north of Nowy Targ, was being bombed. "My father took the tallis and tefilin, and kissed my mother goodbye. 'I'll be back when everything settles down,' he said."

"You are overcome by the quietness of the whole place," said Dina Balbien, recalling the visit she and her daughter Tema made in 1984 to Treblinka, site of the death camp where most of her family from Radom had been destroyed. "It was drizzling when we arrived, and overcast—very quiet and very green—just a field with monuments of stone." Each one of the hundreds upon hundreds of granite memorials represents one of the villages, towns, and cities from which almost a million Jews had been deported to their deaths at Treblinka in 1942 and 1943. "My mother leaned on the Radom stone," Tema remembers, "and talked to her mother, sister, brother, grandparents, and aunt, and other relatives, telling them that she had survived. She said 'goodbye' to them and explained why she hadn't been back for all those years."

Dina's father, Joel Frydman, had been deported to Auschwitz in 1942, and Dina visited the museum there during her five-day stay in Poland. An inquiry she made of the curator of archives produced a document six weeks later, mailed to her home in California. It was a photocopy of her father's ID photo taken upon his entry into Auschwitz. Recorded along with other information was the date of his death: June 25, 1942, less than three weeks after he had arrived. But it was the photograph that shocked her most. "He looks like he had already lost eighty pounds, even though it could have been only a couple of weeks." she said. "You can see his eyes saying, 'We will never survive this inferno.'"

Dina narrowly escaped death several times, usually as the result of luck, she says. In July 1944, two years after her father's death, she and a few hundred other women were sent to Auschwitz from a camp in Pionki, eastern Poland, where they had been working in an ammunition factory. Their fate remained suspended between life and death for about two weeks before Mengele selected some 250 of them to be sent to the city of Hindenburg to work in the shipyards there. Dina, fifteen years old at the time, recalled Mengele's parting words to the group: "You're

Friedka Eishen Goodrich, survivor of the Lodz Ghetto

Dina Balbien (r.) and her daughter, Survivors' Village

lucky! You're the first women to leave Auschwitz through these gates. Everyone else leaves through the chimney!''

Stephanie Clearfield says that a combination of intuition and premonition, plus her small size, accounted for her surviving Auschwitz as a nine-year-old child. She came to the death camp in 1944 among the last deportations from the Lodz Ghetto. "When they came into the barrack for the 'selection,' I would hide," she said. "I could make myself very small." Her parents and her brother and sister all died there. Stephanie was later liberated at Bergen-Belsen. "I remember guards shooting into

Stephanie Clearfield, child survivor of Auschwitz

the barracks on the very day we were liberated. They knew it was all over, but some wanted to kill even then. A little girl was killed this way in the bottom bunk right under where I was—just before the British arrived."

The wonderful ordinariness of her smile as I photographed her at the Gathering, the joyous affect of this woman who is married and has raised two sons—and who owns a sweater-boutique business in suburban Philadelphia—contrasts in an unearthly way with the bit of her past she shared with me. The childhood she describes I cannot imagine. And liberation? What did she feel? "Nothing," she says. "We didn't know *how* to feel. We had lost the ability."

Ilana Lewin and Leon Segen, children of survivors

The Rabbis Leizerowski, father and son

"I dug a ditch under the wire gate," said Leon Schwartzberg. "Another guy and I squeezed under, then ran out into a field." It was April 1945, and the two had just escaped a subsidiary camp of Dachau. "Eventually a farmer saw us. He realized that we were from a concentration camp, so he started to chase us. He chased us with a pitchfork onto a highway. We heard the ground shaking. I said to the other guy—I can't remember his name, but he was from Lodz—'You know, it sounds like tanks!' And then we saw airplanes—thousands of them!—but we didn't know whose they were. I fell to the ground when the planes flew directly overhead, and got a piece of shrapnel in my left knee. My leg felt warm, but I didn't know it was bleeding. . . . The farmer was standing over me with the pitchfork raised, when both of us suddenly saw the first tank—a big, big tank! I saw the white star on it. The farmer ran across the road and into his farmhouse as the tank stopped. An American soldier jumped down and started hugging and kissing me, and asked me, 'You speak English?' I said, 'No.' He then asked if I spoke Polish. 'Yes!' I said. He was from Chicago. His parents were both from Poland, and he spoke a little Polish. I told him what happened. He put me on the tank, took out first aid, put some stuff on my wound, and said, 'You stay here. In about fifteen minutes we will have liberated Landsberg and on the ride back we'll pick you up.' I said, 'I'm afraid. What about the farmer with the pitchfork?' He said, 'Don't worry about it'— and he took out a pistol. 'Come and see what I do with the farmer!' But I said, 'Please don't do it! I've seen enough death—I don't want to see any more!' So he put me back on the tank, and I saw how they took the city. And on the way back he stopped at the farmhouse and said to the farmer, 'Listen! You give him food, you give him everything he needs for as long as he needs to be here—and don't you dare touch him!'"

The farmer and his wife cared for Leon for several days, then he left them and walked to Landsberg, about four miles from the farmer's house in Kaufering. He was feverish and required hospitalization when he arrived. While recuperating, he learned that his sister was alive in Bergen-Belsen. Ten days later, Leon arrived there, only to discover that his wife, too, had been in Bergen-Belsen but had been transported to Sweden for further medical treatment and recuperation just a day earlier! She had been ill with typhus and had been told by a friend of Leon's sister that Leon was dead. "When I heard that he was dead, I went into a coma—and woke up in Sweden," Nadia Schwartzberg recalled.

Nadia was hospitalized in Norrköping for an entire year. Only on her birthday, November 5, 1945, six months after liberation, did she learn that her husband had survived. "I received a letter from him, and a picture that I still carry with me. And in the letter he said, 'I came one day too late.'" Through the efforts of the Hebrew Immigrant Aid Society (HIAS), Leon was reunited with his wife seven months later in Sweden. They stayed in Sweden for six years before immigrating to the United States in 1952 with their five-year-old daughter, Ada. "They are the best memory of my life, the Swedish people!" Nadia said. "I came naked. I didn't have clothes— I didn't have *nothing*. They cared for me totally."

Their second child, Sheila, was born in Philadelphia in 1955. I asked about her earliest memories of being a child of survivors. "I was a young kid, five years old," she said. "My friends had grandparents, aunts and uncles and cousins; and I would look around and never understand why *I* didn't have grandparents. There was a lot of pain, a lot of confusion. I remember nightmares at a very young age—of the Nazis being in our house and killing off my mother, my father, my sister, and cornering me in the basement—and my waking up. It was a recurring dream—I remember running through the whole house, then being in the basement, trying to hide. And there was one point where I used to have dreams and I would wake up and I was strangling myself. Remember the red marks?"—she asked, turning toward her father. ". . . I always asked a lot of questions, and my parents were the

Nadia and Leon Schwartzberg, survivors, with their daughter, Sheila

kind of people who would tell me. I don't think it made sense to me, you know . . . but I listened to it. It was important, even then, to learn what my heritage was. Sometimes, of course, I feel very removed from it—like I don't believe this happened. I'm looking at my parents, and I don't believe—I *can't* believe—that they went through what they did, and survived."

Late in the summer of 1942, Erwin Baum, age twelve, returned to his orphanage in the Warsaw Ghetto just past dawn after a night of begging. Everyone was gone. As far as he has been able to determine, he is the only survivor of Dr. Janusz Korczak's Orphans' Home. "Dr. Korczak was someone the Germans offered freedom to, but he refused. He was director of the orphanage, a physician, and a writer—and the only Jew who had [before the war] a program on radio," Erwin said. Radio listeners referred to him with fond respect as "The Old Doctor."

Erwin and Anna Baum, survivors

A major in the Polish Army, Korczak was well known as an imaginative and progressive educator, the originator of a famous children's newspaper in pre-war Poland, and a firmly independent thinker. "He refused the passport, saying he needed 120 more—for all of his kids," Erwin said. "So they sent him to Treblinka." With all of his kids, ages seven to eighteen. Unable to save his children, he chose to be with them until the very end. Thirty-five years earlier, he had made another

Survivors, Highland Park (New Jersey)

very conscious choice: not to marry and raise children of his own but to serve instead the cause of children in every way possible. It was this sixty-four-year-old man whom Vladka Meed saw from the window of her hiding place in the ghetto that day in August 1942. She witnessed the tight formation of orphans, hand-in-hand, being marched by German soldiers to the cattle cars that would take them to their deaths in Treblinka. The youngest were in front, led by their trusted "father," Janusz Korczak. "Certainly," his Polish biographer, Alicja Szlazakowa, wrote, "for the first time in his life, the doctor did not tell them the truth."

The orphan who missed this deportation, Erwin Baum, survived several camps before being liberated by American troops near Dachau. He is pictured here in Survivors' Village, wearing his ID photo from 1945 on the sign around his neck. He remembers being so starved by the time of his liberation that he jumped onto an American army truck and got sick gorging himself on chocolate, so sick that he had to be hospitalized in Mildorf, a town near Munich. He spent two weeks there, long enough to be able to walk again, then went on his own into Munich, where he stayed about a year.

Erwin's wife, Anna, survived the Holocaust hidden by Christians in the basement of their home in Slutsk, a town near Minsk in the Soviet Union. They hid several other children as well, for four years. Today Anna works as a designer of ladies' jackets, and Erwin owns a secondhand fur and antique clothing shop in New York.

Eva Pasternak, survivor of Auschwitz

"What would you like for this beautiful work?" Eva Pasternak was asked, as she handed the silk blouse to the SS supervisor who had ordered it made for her birthday. Eva had been repairing and altering clothes and uniforms for SS women in the Muehlhausen-Thuringen slave labor camp, which supplied workers for an underground ammunition factory about three miles away in the forest. She had responded right away when the same SS supervisor asked a month earlier whether anyone among the 300 inmates could sew well. "That saved my life," Eva said.

Late afternoon at the Civic Center, last day of the Gathering

"The sewing machine was in a separate room in one of the barracks of the camp, so I no longer had to undergo the hour-and-a-half march to and from the factory. I had been operating a drill press machine there." Until evacuation four months later, she remained the camp's seamstress, altering the uniforms and doing some "private work" as well, such as the blouse. "Her husband was some high-ranking SS officer, and he had sent her a beautiful piece of eggshell-white silk and some lace for her birthday," Eva said. "She had seen how good my work was, so she wanted me to make her a blouse."

What did Eva answer when the SS supervisor asked what she would like? Eva remembers being stunned at first by the absurdity of their situation. "Do *I* have a *choice*? Do *I* have a choice *here*?!" she asked her. "With *me* you have," the supervisor responded, "because you have golden hands." Eva then made her

Charles and Tola Zuckerman at the Civic Center

request: "If you could bring me a toothbrush. . . ." She hadn't brushed her teeth for four years. "But if somebody would see that you have a toothbrush," the supervisor objected, "then *my* life is in danger. We're not supposed to do that—or to mix with you *at all*." But the supervisor brought her the toothbrush. "And every once in a while she brought me a piece of bread, or I got the biggest soup, you know? She said she had never seen a blouse so beautiful. 'And don't worry,' she told me. 'When we win the war I will see to it that you work in the biggest fashion house in Berlin.' In my heart I said to myself, 'I would rather die. But you will not win the war—God would not be so cruel as to let *that* happen.'"

Eva was ten years old in 1940 when her family was forced into the ghetto from their home in Lodz. In the spring of 1944, she married her sweetheart, Melvin, who

Woman outside the Civic Center

was ten years older than she. "My husband thought he could protect me by marrying me." Three months later they were shipped to Auschwitz and she never saw him again. "At fourteen, I was probably the youngest widow in the world," she said.

In the beginning of March 1945, Eva ended up in Bergen-Belsen, one among the fewer than fifty of the decimated population of the slave-labor camp arriving from the Thuringen region. "I saw mountains of dead bodies, mountains and

Mania Drelich, survivor, Skokie (Illinois), with her grandson, Alex

mountains! The stench of human flesh, typhoid, so many lice you could catch them in your hand." She saw some Russian prisoners of war so starved that they resorted to eating human flesh, opening up the bodies of the dead. "When the SS found out what had happened and who did it, they hanged them. But for what *they* did, the Nazis, creating such a hell—*that* was okay! They took us out from the barracks and made us watch how they hanged them."

When liberation came six weeks later, Eva remembers not being able to feel

Woman and children boarding bus for National Museum

anything at the restoration of her freedom. "I was so helpless, so down-broken . . . so abandoned. All of us survivors, we had no strength to be happy. We were *immune* to every feeling. Nothing could affect us anymore." She was six months away from her sixteenth birthday. "You can imagine how I looked: blue skin and bones, without any hair. I weighed only forty-five pounds. . . . I said that I would never look in the mirror again in my life. It's amazing how much a human being can take."

I met Anne Stern on the last day of the Gathering as she was boarding a bus to the final activity—an event at the National Museum of American Jewish History. Like many others that weekend, she wanted to know why I was taking photographs. So I told her my story. Then she told me hers, and I learned that she too had been three years old at the time of the liberation of the camps in 1945. She was a child survivor.

"You're the child I've been searching for all weekend!" I exclaimed, embracing her. We were both forty-three years old, born in 1942, just three months apart—I in Philadelphia, she in Szeged, a city in southern Hungary. At the time of her birth, the Jews there were already living in a ghetto. In May 1942, before his newborn daughter was even two weeks old, her father, Tibor Grunberger, a twenty-nine-year-old dentist, was deported to a forced-labor camp in the Ukraine. Anne's mother was left in the ghetto with the new baby and her four-year-old son, Ferenc. They remained in Szeged until May 1944, when all three were sent to Wiener Neustadt, a labor camp in eastern Austria, then to Theresienstadt (Terezin), Czechoslovakia, early in June. Most of the other members of her family—including her grandparents, a great-grandmother, and many uncles, aunts, and cousins—had meanwhile been sent to concentration camps in Poland, where all perished.

Theresienstadt, proclaimed a "model ghetto" by the Germans, received its first deportations from Prague in the fall of 1941. Already, by the end of January·1942, it functioned as it would for the next two and a half years, primarily as a transit to the gas chambers of Auschwitz and Majdanek. It is estimated that more than 120,000 deaths occurred through this Theresienstadt-Auschwitz-Majdanek connection during that time—more than 80,000 through deportations to Auschwitz alone from Theresienstadt, of which more than 15,000 were children. Anne and her brother are among only one hundred child survivors of Theresienstadt. They were liberated by Russian troops on May 8, 1945, five days after Anne's third birthday.

"My mother saved our lives," Anne wrote me in a letter, months after the Gathering. "She cleaned hospital grounds, took care of sick people, carried bricks to build houses—the work of three persons in order to keep us with her in the same camp. I never could understand how she managed it. Thus we were not taken to Auschwitz where the major part of my family was gassed."

Anne remembers their coming back to Hungary right after liberation, and their reunion with an aunt who had been hidden in basements during the last months of the war. "I was three years old and weighed a little less than twenty pounds. My mother was carrying me in her arms as I couldn't walk, and she finally got to her sister's place in Budapest . . . and when her sister opened the door, she simply put me in her arms and collapsed. . . . I was a year in hospitals between life and death, as at the age of three I had decided I was not willing to live anymore." Her father also survived and rejoined them in Budapest, but for a long time Anne remained too ill and devoid of spirit to regard him as anything but a stranger at her bedside. "Again my mother, by walking me along the streets in a stroller, succeeded in bringing me back to life again. I didn't walk for a year, then finally I began to smile and to walk again."

Anne's good fortune in surviving Theresienstadt was rare, but rarer still was the survival as well of her only sibling and both parents. They stayed in Hungary until the Revolution in 1956 and spent one year afterward in refugee camps in Yugoslavia. The family then immigrated to Switzerland where Anne continued her studies, as well as her special interest in languages—Hungarian, French, and Spanish. Her father resumed his professional career as a dentist, and her brother completed many years of study and training to become a pharmacist. Her father died in 1983 at the age of seventy—the age her mother, Veronika, just reached this past year.

"Five years ago I was lucky to have been introduced to my husband, Bart, also a survivor," Anne wrote. "He had spent one year in Jaworzno, near Auschwitz,

Anne Stern, child survivor of Theresienstadt

and was liberated by the Russians in Birkenau on the 27th of January, 1945—a few meters from the gas chamber, hidden under dead bodies. He was then eighteen years old. Being an Orthodox Jew, his faith helped him to stay alive. We were married in Geneva . . . on February 7, 1982, five weeks after our first meeting, and we give thanks to G-d for having brought us together." Anne moved to Los Angeles to live with her husband and his two children, Jonathan, nineteen, and Nina, seventeen.

"As we have been so fortunate to survive," Anne wrote, "we think that we are here to do something. We should be thankful to G-d, and the best way to do so is to show that we care for others. This is our aim, and this makes our life together more meaningful and worthwhile." Recently, Anne told me that she and Bart had just received formal approval of their application to become foster parents. "Now we will be able to offer a home to some children desperately needing it." I couldn't help thinking of the 15,000 children of Theresienstadt—and more than a million other children who had desperately needed refuge during the years of the Holocaust, but were enveloped instead by the Einsatzgruppen, the Gestapo, the death camps.

Several weeks later, Anne sent me a photograph that her mother had recently discovered and mailed to her from Switzerland. Taken in Budapest in 1946, it is the earliest photo of Anne's family reunited after the war. It is a luminous portrait of life recovered, yet one can see in it the evidence of suffering and loss as surely as one sees, in the photograph of me on my tricycle that same year, the image of a life unthreatened.

I end with Anne's story because it is where mine begins, and where we can begin, together, to talk and to grow. Your generation, Mark and Justine, is our hope for continued, deeper healing. The process is a long one, begun only in recent years. It involves creating more bridges for dialogue, often across painful religious, ethnic, and political boundaries. It also means converting our insights into efforts on behalf of today's refugees and victims of oppression, whatever their race, religion, nationality. It means remembering the terrible consequences of indifference.

As you continue to grow and to find your own ways of bearing witness, be encouraged by the example of these survivors whose lives now touch yours. And so be hopeful, despite the darkness of the past, despite those who may seek to undermine your efforts, and despite your own imperfect vision. Always remember that the one thing in this world greater than the human capacity for evil is our capacity for good.

Love,
Dad

Anne with her parents and brother, Budapest, 1946

Afterword

On a bright and sunny day early in the fall of 1987, Bernard Stehle stood at the door of my office with a thick black binder under his arm. In it were the photographs carefully selected for his latest book, *Another Kind of Witness*. I had often talked with Bernard as a fellow member of the Interfaith Council on the Holocaust. But this time, after a brief greeting, he had a specific question in mind: Would I review the photographs, read the accompanying manuscript, and consider writing an afterword to his book?

How would this book be different from the numerous other volumes I had read about Holocaust survivors? It would be different because the author was not himself a survivor; he was a comparatively young man, a father, and a Christian. He would tell the stories of Jewish survivors he had met at the American Gathering in 1985 through the eyes of a Christian. Convinced that he had a special mission, he had spent hours interviewing survivors and capturing their images on film. His photographs would present the reader with men and women today, forty years after Auschwitz, juxtaposed with his retelling of their miraculous stories of suffering and survival.

What better way for a Christian author to confront the Holocaust than by becoming the voices of its survivors, by presenting us with images of real people, modern Americans, whose suffering is almost unfathomable? Libraries are filled with historical texts describing the Hitler era. Mountains of information have been disseminated concerning the events that transpired between the years 1933 and 1945. But, despite the numbers of books that have been written, I dare say, that many hearts remain untouched by the incomprehensible event known to our twentieth century as the Holocaust. Arm-chair philosophers have noted that the shortest distance in life between two places is really the longest journey—the distance between the mind and the heart. *Another Kind of Witness* shortens the distance considerably. It touches the heart in a unique and special way.

The question that Mark poses to his father at the beginning of the book recalls another scene of a father and son in dialogue, the Passover Seder. The child's question at the Seder calls forth the telling of a story that will not only touch the heart of the child but will also long be remembered. It is the story of a journey from slavery to freedom that is retold and relived perennially. Like the child at the Seder, Mark asks the difficult question: "Why?" The "what" and the "when" questions come first and are easily handled. The "why" questions are often the imponderables that stay with us and cause considerable uneasiness! "But if the Holocaust was going on for that long," Mark asks his father, "why didn't anybody do something about it?"

Another Kind of Witness will not resolve the question or put it to rest. The stories reveal the best and the worst in human behavior. Raoul Wallenberg, Jan Karski, and others are portrayed as the "Righteous Gentiles" they were. They are presented as caring individuals who tried to do something, and did. They responded positively to the age old Biblical question, "Am I my brother's (sister's) keeper?"

Youthful readers can relate to another aspect of the question in Vladka Meed's remembrance of the youth in the Warsaw Ghetto: ". . . they were youth who lived with certain ideals, with certain beliefs. And this sustained them during the ghetto time." While those who might have been able to help often remained passive bystanders, young people from the ghettos did something about their situation and stayed the hand of the enemy in incredible ways.

On the darker side, stories of prejudice and betrayal by Christians against Jews sharpen the question, "Why didn't anybody do something about it?" They give rise to further questions—questions concerning the relationships of Jews and Christians over the centuries, certainly not a relationship of brotherly love! This is good. The questions need to be raised because many Christians know far too little about the history of Christian anti-Semitism.

Bernard Stehle's work is an invaluable contribution to the ongoing challenge of Holocaust education. Many readers will come to grips, perhaps for the first time, with the extent of Jewish suffering. In telling the story of the Jews who survived, the author brings his readers face to face with the millions who perished. His own identification with the survivors as he tells their stories rings true for the reader. Yet Stehle brings his work to a close in a spirit of hope, encouraging his readers to take heart. He enjoins us to take up the task of becoming bridgebuilders in this age of dialogue between Christians and Jews so that never again will history be allowed to repeat itself.

Another Kind of Witness is truly a book for everyone. Its message cannot fail, and surely it will shorten that longest journey in life—the journey from the head to the heart! That is no small contribution.

Sister Gloria Coleman, SHCJ

Sister Gloria Coleman is Coordinator for Ecumenical and Interfaith Affairs, Cardinal's Commission on Human Relations, Archdiocese of Philadelphia, and Honorary Chairperson, Interfaith Council on the Holocaust, Philadelphia.

Acknowledgments

Without the initial support and on-going commitment of the Association of Jewish Holocaust Survivors in Philadelphia—especially Abram Shnaper, President of the Association—this book would never have been possible. In his tireless, quietly resourceful way, Abram coordinated the plans to see two Philadelphia exhibitions of "Another Kind of Witness" to their memorable opening nights. I have continued to benefit ever since from his wise counsel and friendship.

For their generous work on the exhibitions that resulted in this book, I thank Myrna Amsel and Florence Kaufman of the Charles and Elizabeth Gershman YM&YWHA, and Phyllis Apparies of the Raymond and Miriam Klein Branch, of Jewish Community Centers of Greater Philadelphia. Additional sponsors of the exhibition in the Klein Center's Fred Wolf Jr. Gallery include the Sons and Daughters of Holocaust Survivors in Philadelphia, the Memorial Committee for the Six Million Jewish Martyrs, The Jewish Times, Community College of Philadelphia, and Arnold and Esther Tuzman. Other sponsors of the earlier show at the Gershman "Y" include the National Museum of American Jewish History, who provided the extra wall panels we needed, and the Pennsylvania Humanities Council, whose grant to the Association of Jewish Holocaust Survivors in Philadelphia helped meet exhibition expenses. For a special grant from the Office of Arts and Culture of the City of Philadelphia, I wish to thank Oliver Franklin, the Deputy City Representative.

I owe a continuing debt of gratitude to Dr. Samuel Laeuchli, professor of Religion at Temple University and director of the MIMESIS Institute of Religion, Myth, and the Healing Arts, and to Dr. Evelyn Rothchild, clinical psychologist, who have been valued consultants and friends during several stages of the evolution of this work. Special thanks to Bjorn Krondorfer of the German-Jewish Dance Theater for sharing his ideas with me on several occasions during the writing of the text. The efforts of this small troupe of dancers, made up of Jews and Gentiles who interpret the living implications and historical issues of the Holocaust through modern dance, are an important example of dialogue occurring between young Germans and Jews today.

Thanks also to Jean Russell for her generous loan given spontaneously to me one afternoon in her son Luke's garden in Philadelphia; visiting from Tucson, Arizona, six months after the Gathering, she made it possible for me to obtain the seventy 16″ × 20″ contact sheets of the photographs I had taken at the Gathering. It was these contact sheets that I showed to Abram Shnaper one week later, at the suggestion of Nora Levin—thus initiating the whole process leading to the exhibitions and book.

I am indebted to Professor Nora Levin for her dedicated work as director of the Holocaust Oral History archive at Gratz College, from which I have drawn in my efforts to understand the Holocaust and complete my work on this book. For historical grounding and facts, I have relied heavily on her 1968 volume (paperback edition, 1973), *The Holocaust: The Destruction of European Jewry, 1933–1945*, and on the work of Martin Gilbert, especially *The Holocaust: A History of the Jews of Europe During the Second World War* (1985) and *The Macmillan Atlas of the Holocaust* (1982). While acknowledging the works of these two authorities on the Holocaust, I remain responsible for any errors of fact or judgment which the final text may yet contain.

Many other books have added much to my continuing efforts to grasp the history and implications of the Holocaust, but my primary sources for this text have been my conversations with survivors. It is their stories that fill these pages and that no other history can fully approach; I regret that I have been unable to recount all of them. For those included, I hope only that I have been a faithful recorder and editor of the extraordinary accounts that have been shared with me during the past two years. Although I have tried to review carefully with each one the final text of their accounts as told to me, I hold only myself responsible for any faults in the final rendering. Special appreciation goes to Roman Kent and Benjamin Meed, of the American Gathering and Federation of Jewish Holocaust Survivors, who provided me with helpful information and insight during the final stages of the manuscript, and to Lawrence Y. Goldberg, executive director of the Philadelphia Gathering.

For his readiness always to help clarify a point of vocabulary or syntax with me, I thank my friend, Richard Serano. Other individuals who contributed their ideas, time, and generosity in many forms, and without whom these exhibitions and book could not have occurred, include Arnold Shay, Menachem Kozuch, Clara Isaacman, Harry Bass, Luba Shnaper and Isadore Hollander of the Association of Jewish Holocaust Survivors in Philadelphia; Barbara Klaczynska, Joseph Barish, Geoffrey Berken, Anthony Wychunis and Carl Quandt of Community College of Philadelphia; Henning Hansen of the University of Lund, Sweden; and Rick Willens, Jana Mossey, James H. Allen, Susan Romberger, Elizabeth Turner and Heddy Bergsman. My thanks as well to students of the Photography Department of Community College who assisted me with the production of prints for the exhibitions: Michael Fantini, Laurie Myer, Martin Lennon, Carol Sykes, Rosa La Rocca, David DiDonato, Charmaine Mack, Amanda Stevenson and Susan Dougherty.

Other relatives, friends, and colleagues who have assisted in numerous supportive ways on this project include Robert Hufford, Sr., Ed Stehle, Lorraine Sawyer, James M. Crowley, Judith Stehle, William and Theresa West, Greg Pomeroy, Philip Taylor, Tom O'Hara, Valerie Polin and Robert Langmuir, Gerry and Lorraine Givnish, Eva Stehle, and Luke Russell. Special thanks go to Mary DeWitt—painter, teacher, listener—for being there again and again with loving care, helpful suggestions, and continuing dialogue. To my parents, Ruth and Bernard F. Stehle, Sr., I give a son's special tribute for their unquestioning support, both spiritually and materially, throughout this project.

For the past year, no one has been more patient and receptive to ideas, suggestions, changes—in her always positive, insightful, and open manner—than Sheila Segal, my editor at the Jewish Publication Society. I am grateful to her for creating the kind of vital, freely critical yet supportive atmosphere that allowed us to work together on a project of this kind with its special sensitivities and coordination of efforts and concerns of a number of different individuals and organizations. My appreciation also goes to Nathan Barnett, formerly executive vice president of JPS; to Barbara Spector, formerly managing editor; and to Philip and Muriel Berman, whose endowment fund made the publication of this book possible.

I am indebted to my children, Mark and Justine, for their honesty and for the challenge they present to me intellectually and morally as we do history together in and outside our separate classrooms, seeking one another's viewpoints as we go about our individual projects. What they have helped me to confront during these past two years in particular is reflected in the pages of this book.

Bernard F. Stehle